The
FRIENDSHIP
BOOK

of Francis Gay

A THOUGHT
FOR EACH DAY
IN 2007

D. C. THOMSON & CO., LTD.
London Glasgow Manchester Dundee

Friends are quiet angels who lift us to our feet when our wings have trouble remembering how to fly.

January

MONDAY — JANUARY 1.

AT the beginning of another New Year the Lady of the House and I send you a bouquet of the roses of life, golden moments of serenity and friendship, love and happiness, joy and good health.

The best of New Years to you all!

TUESDAY — JANUARY 2.

ELLEN is a violinist. For many years she was a member of a renowned symphony orchestra, but has now settled into happy semi-retirement, teaching a few keen and talented pupils.

"And yet," she said, "as a youngster, I hardly dared hope that I'd ever be able to make music my profession. I came from a family with little money to spare, and knew no-one who made their living as a musician. But then a friend told me of some words spoken by former American President, Woodrow Wilson.

"He said that you should never allow hope to die. You should 'nurse your dreams and protect them through bad times and tough times to the sunshine and light which always come'. And now, I'm glad I did!"

Often other people's dreams can make a better world for all of us.

WEDNESDAY — JANUARY 3.

GEORGE has always been a keen gardener, so I suppose I shouldn't have been surprised by his sudden pronouncement that New Year resolutions always made him think of vegetables.

"Well, you see," he explained, "some folk seem to think that simply planting the seed is enough, and all they have to do after that is to sit back. They don't seem to realise that to produce good results, both plants and resolutions need plenty of nurturing."

I must admit that I had never thought of resolutions that way before — but I'll try to remember to tend my resolutions just as often as I water my plants!

THURSDAY — JANUARY 4.

ISN'T the old saying "You only hurt the ones you love" so often all too true? It's sometimes easy to be short-tempered with those closest to us, in a way that we'd never be with a stranger or casual acquaintance. We know our friends and family will love us anyway, but is it fair to take advantage of that?

When everything seems to be going wrong, we might not feel like being cheerful, but as the actress, poet and author Maya Angelou says, "If you have only one smile in you, give it to the people you love. Don't be surly at home, then go out in the street and start grinning 'Good morning' at total strangers."

That's something to think about the next time we feel a frown coming on!

FRIDAY — JANUARY 5.

WE sometimes forget, I think, to give enough thanks for the sudden appearance of a rainbow in the sky.

The vision is so breathtaking. Seen after a storm, this wonder of nature adds a sparkle to the day. I remember Rachel, a friend's daughter, calling excitedly to us:

"Look up, please," she shouted. "Oh, I never knew before that orange could go so well with purple. It's wonderful!"

I also recall a favourite wish, origin unknown, which expresses this hope: "May we never miss a sunset or a rainbow because we are looking down."

SATURDAY — JANUARY 6.

MY friend Ralph is a banker with years of experience but he is also a man with strong religious beliefs and has no high opinion of money. "It will buy you expensive things," he said, "but not happiness.

"Money can do a power of good, but it won't wipe the frown from a miserable face or patch up a broken friendship. Even a million pounds won't buy a contented heart," he continued.

And who better to make that point than a man with Ralph's background.

SUNDAY — JANUARY 7.

SALVATION belongeth unto the Lord: thy blessing is upon thy people.

Psalms 3:8

MONDAY — JANUARY 8.

AFTER my Great-Aunt Louisa had enjoyed a visit from her cousin Paul, his wife Helen and their children, she wrote in her diary:

"8th January — Snow softly blankets the countryside, and it is very quiet except for Sarah and David playing in the garden. They are so excited, for living in India they have seldom seen snow. They have built a snowman, helped their father to clear the garden paths and, just a few moments ago when I went to call them in for lunch, I saw them both lying spreadeagled in the snow, arms and legs outstreched in an X-shape. They shouted to me:

"'Look at us, Aunt Louisa, we're making angels in the snow!'

"Not windmills or crosses, but angels — I rather like that. What was it the poet Francis Thompson wrote? *The angels keep their ancient places.* A rather comforting thought. I like the idea of guardian angels; they speak of God's concern for us."

TUESDAY — JANUARY 9.

THE GOOD SHEPHERD

THE Lord my pasture shall prepare,
And feed me with a shepherd's care;
His presence shall my wants supply,
And guard me with a watchful eye;
My noonday walks he shall attend,
And all my midnight hours defend.

Joseph Addison (1672-1719).

WEDNESDAY — JANUARY 10.

HAVE you ever been introduced to a stranger, only to form an instant impression of dislike? We sometimes find ourselves having to spend time with someone with whom we feel little or no affinity.

These are the occasions when we really need to persevere, for often we'll discover that as our knowledge of a person grows, so our antagonism shrinks, until we are surprised to recall that we ever disliked them. With luck, we may even find that we have made a lasting friendship.

THURSDAY — JANUARY 11.

"WHAT a friend we have in Jesus" has always been a popular hymn, so I was fascinated to learn the story behind the words. It was penned by an Irishman, Joseph Scriven, who seemed to have been born to every worldly blessing until, on the eve of his wedding, his fiancée was tragically drowned.

Finding that only his Christian faith gave him the strength to carry on, he started to live a different kind of life, donating freely both his time and possessions to help those in need. He wrote his well-loved hymn as a poem for his mother, to comfort her during illness, and this extract plainly expresses the faith and thankfulness of which he never lost sight.

What a friend we have in Jesus,
All our sins and griefs to bear!
What a privilege to carry
Everything to God in prayer!

FRIDAY — JANUARY 12.

A GREAT many people nowadays sometimes feel a need for silence. Our lives are so hectic, so hurried that there seems to be little time left to be quiet, no space to hear that "still small voice" which speaks to our inner being.

Some folk find it while out walking in the hills, some while sailing the seas, or just sitting quietly by the fireside on a Winter's evening. Others find it in prayer and meditation.

But to many, silence is alienating: every moment, it seems, must be filled with noise and movement.

Silence is, though, so much more than the absence of noise. Silence is music asleep. Find it and you will find that "peace which passes all understanding".

SATURDAY — JANUARY 13.

THE social reformer, surgeon, and writer, Samuel Smiles, wrote these words in the 19th century:

"Self-respect is the noblest garment with which man may clothe himself — the most elevating feeling with which the mind can be inspired."

An excellent thought for today. Let's remember it!

SUNDAY — JANUARY 14.

A ND on the seventh day God ended his work which he had made; and he rested on the seventh day from all his work which he had made.

Genesis 2:2

MONDAY — JANUARY 15.

I'VE been reading about Voltaire, the French writer and philosopher. Born in 1694, he was a witty but ruthless critic of the corrupt ruling powers of his era; a man whose refusal to ignore injustice not only offended the authorities, but also led to periods of imprisonment and exile.

His was a turbulent existence, so I was not surprised to read that he once described life as "a shipwreck". What I did find admirable was his further comment that nevertheless, "we must not forget to sing in the lifeboats".

That's the sort of shipmate we could all do with.

TUESDAY — JANUARY 16.

THE journey of the Spirit
Is one we make alone,
A journey needing fortitude
The pathway quite unknown.
Though loving thoughts go with us
Each mile that we begin,
We need new courage, faith and hope
To warm us deep within.

No-one knows how steep the road
And no-one knows the length,
But as we travel on our way
We grow in inner strength.
The journey of the Spirit
Continues day and night,
Beyond the darkness and the pain
To reach Eternal Light.

Iris Hesselden.

WEDNESDAY — JANUARY 17.

A MAN wrote to a newspaper saying, "I think I'll stop going to church. I have gone for thirty years and heard thousands of sermons, yet can't remember any of them. I've been wasting my time."

Another churchgoer wrote back: "I have been married for thirty years. In that time my wife has cooked thousands of meals. I don't remember any of them, but they nourished me and gave me strength. Without them I would be dead, and without hearing a sermon every week I would be spiritually dead."

The first man continued to go to church.

THURSDAY — JANUARY 18.

O UR friend Keith was visiting a city centre high-rise office block, and in the midst of all the hustle and bustle, the rushing of people to and fro, he came across this notice on a wall:

The right time to relax is when you don't have time for it.

A simple message, but with words worth taking time to consider now.

FRIDAY — JANUARY 19.

W HENEVER I see squirrels digging up the nuts they buried the previous Autumn, it makes me think of human beings in possession of good things. We, too, can keep stored all the special and important moments that have been ours, and dig them out once more in the darker days when we feel downhearted.

SATURDAY — JANUARY 20.

OUR friend Peter related this favourite story one day. I'm not sure how accurate it is but the message is crystal clear.

Engineers were laying the final sections that would complete the links between the two sides of the Forth Railway Bridge. But they were too short. The holes in the girders were some distance from the holes they would need to match before the bolts could slide through.

But no one panicked. Instead they waited as the rising sun shone on their mammoth project, warming the metal and expanding the bridge. A couple of hours later those vital bolts slipped smoothly into place.

A fine example of what can be achieved by spreading a little sunshine on a difficult situation.

SUNDAY — JANUARY 21.

DELIGHT thyself also in the Lord; and he shall give thee the desires of thine heart.

Psalms 37:4

MONDAY — JANUARY 22.

HERE are some wise words from the 18th-century Methodist clergyman John Wesley:
Do all the good you can,
By all the means you can,
In all the ways you can,
In all the places you can.
At all the times you can,
To all the people you can
As long as ever you can.

TUESDAY — JANUARY 23.

NEVER let opportunities pass you by. After all, "small opportunities are often the beginning of great enterprises".

Those are the words of the famous Greek orator Demosthenes who was born in 384 B.C.

Words well worth remembering.

WEDNESDAY — JANUARY 24.

FATHER, always go with me;
Take my ears that they would hear
Your instruction loud and clear.
Take my eyes that they would see
All your children equally.
Take my mouth that it would speak
Truth and wisdom, bold yet meek.
Take my heart that it would mourn
With the broken and forlorn.
Take my hands that they would bear
Gracious solace everywhere.
Take my feet that they would bring
Assurance to the faltering.
Father, this I ask of Thee,
Wherever you may gently lead
Ever, always go with me.

Rachel Wallace-Oberle.

THURSDAY — JANUARY 25.

OLD friends are like diamonds
Precious and rare.
New friends are like Autumn leaves
Found everywhere.

FRIDAY — JANUARY 26.

WHILE driving past a church, our friend Ian noticed that the clergyman had put up this notice: *Will the road you're on get you to God's house?*

What a thought-provoking question! It reminds me of a friend who carries a small Bible in her handbag because, as she says, "I like to have the road map for the journey at my fingertips."

SATURDAY — JANUARY 27.

MY friend Henry likes to surprise me with new information. "You are interested in words, Francis," he said one day. "Well, do you know an English word which owes its existence to Roman potters?"

I shook my head, but he went on to explain that potters might throw a pot which was cracked. They filled the crack with wax, painted it over, but when warm liquid was poured in, the wax melted and there was a leak.

Good potters advertised that their pots were *sine cera* — "without wax" — and, in time, *sine cera* developed into the word we know as "sincerely".

To be sincere means, literally, that you are not waxing over your imperfections. No wonder the study of words can be fascinating!

SUNDAY — JANUARY 28.

GRACE be with all them that love our Lord Jesus Christ in sincerity. Amen.

Ephesians 6:24

MONDAY — JANUARY 29.

MAHATMA Gandhi once pronounced that the logic of an eye for an eye and a tooth for a tooth cannot sustain itself forever; sooner or later both parties end up blind and toothless.

Why do we never seem to learn?

TUESDAY — JANUARY 30.

THERE'S nothing quite like nostalgia at times, and how often our memories are kindled by something as simple as a smell.

I know one young man who cheerfully breathes in the smell of country fields whenever he is out rambling, and he is then transported back to idyllic childhood holidays on his grandparents' farm.

Jan, who often travelled on steam trains as a child, took a trip on one not long ago and declared it "wonderful!" And what did she enjoy most about the experience? The smell she had hated as a child!

Though time moves on, the memories remain. Perhaps the nineteenth-century Irish poet and songwriter Thomas Moore said it best:

*You may break, you may shatter, the vase
if you will,
But the scent of the roses will hang round it still.*

WEDNESDAY — JANUARY 31.

HERE is a thought for today on happiness: "A happy person is not a person in a certain set of circumstances, but rather a person with a certain set of attitudes."

BRIGHT LIGHT

February

GOD loves an expectant heart. Package your prayers in trust, stamp them with confidence and send them by faith!

I THINK I will call this a small February miscellany. One late Winter's day as the light faded, our neighbour John lingered in his garden, appreciative of that subtle, but noticeable lengthening of the light which comes in February.

Candlemas Day, 2nd February, is positioned mid-way between the shortest day and the Spring Equinox, and marks the beginning of the Easter season in the Christian calendar.

Perhaps, then, it was fitting that he noticed a pasque flower was beginning to unfurl its ferny green leaves in preparation for its later flowering.

And for those with a February birthday, an unknown writer said:

The February born will find
Sincerity and peace of mind;
Freedom from passion and from care,
If they the pearl will wear.

So ends these reflections on a month which takes its name from a Roman festival of purification, *Februa*.

SATURDAY — FEBRUARY 3.

I ONCE read the story of a woman who could no longer stand the chaos of her existence. Then, in a dream, an angel showed her a beautiful tapestry of her life.

"That's how it should be," she exclaimed.

"That's how it is," the angel replied, turning the tapestry around and revealing the confusion of coloured threads that made up the completed picture. "You're just looking at it from the wrong side."

The memory of those threads came back to me when I read these words by Simone Signoret — "Chains do not hold a marriage together," she said. "It is threads, hundreds of tiny threads which sew people together through the years."

In both stories I'm sure the stitches were made with love.

SUNDAY— FEBRUARY 4.

AND the whole earth was of one language, and of one speech.

Genesis 11:1

MONDAY — FEBRUARY 5.

BORN in 1809 in a log-cabin in Kentucky, Abraham Lincoln rose to be President of the United States of America. He gave young people everywhere these two fine challenges:

"Do your own growing, no matter how tall your grandfather was."

"Whatever you are, be a good one."

Two practical thoughts for us to consider.

TUESDAY — FEBRUARY 6.

*M*AY the strength of the hills
  Give you courage,
The calm of still waters
  Give you peace.
The joyfulness of nature
  Give you hope,
And the wonder of the seasons
  Never cease.

May the beauty of the morning
  Lift depression,
The quiet of the evening
  Give you rest,
The voyage of your life
  Be smooth and tranquil,
And all the days ahead
  Be truly blessed.
        Iris Hesselden.

WEDNESDAY — FEBRUARY 7.

WHEN asked for a principle by which to conduct life Confucius replied, "Do not do to others what you do not want them to do to you." In this context Prophet Mohammed said, "He is not a believer who does not love for his brother what he loves for himself." While in Sikh scripture we are urged to "treat others as thou wouldst be treated thyself".

Both the Torah and the Bible contain the words: "Love your neighbour as yourself."

Varied as the world's religions might be, it seems that we're more alike than we may realise.

THE AWAKENING

THURSDAY — FEBRUARY 8.

IT'S a rare, and perhaps incomplete, life that hasn't known loss. I'd like to share these words in the hope that they might help someone.

"Our spirit," wrote the philosopher Johann Wolfgang von Goethe, "is indestructible and continues from eternity to eternity. It is like the sun, which seems to set only to our earthly eyes, but which, in reality, shines on unceasingly."

Richard Bach, the author of "Jonathan Livingston Seagull" had this to say on the moment of final separation: "Remember, what the caterpillar calls a tragedy, the Master calls a butterfly."

FRIDAY — FEBRUARY 9.

I CAME across a spiritual "wish list" one day. The unknown compiler had included the following:

A little common sense, to take people as they are, not how I think they should be.

A little more cheerfulness, to share my happiness rather than my sorrows.

A little more humility, to do God's work when I'd rather be looking to my own comfort.

A little more perseverance, to keep doing the above.

A little more prayer, to leave a space in my heart where God can speak and I can listen.

It struck me how much of a difference "a little" can make. And the wonder of it is that each and every one of us, no matter how rich or poor, has it in us to do "a little" of the truly important things.

SATURDAY — FEBRUARY 10.

CHANGES were being made to our local library and I had obviously voiced my misgivings once too often, for the next time I mentioned the subject the Lady of the House was well prepared.

"I've found two quotations to cheer you up," she told me. "The first is from Pauline R. Kezer who said that although 'continuity gives us roots, change gives us branches, letting us stretch and grow and reach new heights'."

"I like that," I said. "And the other one?"

She laughed. "It's from a writer called Robert Gallagher. 'Change is inevitable — except from a vending machine'."

SUNDAY — FEBRUARY 11.

JESUS said unto him, If thou canst believe, all things are possible to him that believeth.

Mark 9: 23

MONDAY — FEBRUARY 12.

DURING the General Assembly of the Church of Scotland in 2002, the gathering was enhanced by "children's ambassadors" in recognition and celebration of "The Year Of The Child". The young ones were thrilled to be there and to help lead the opening prayers.

The then Moderator still likes to recall a petition made by one little girl: "We pray for the Moderator, Finlay Macdonald, that he may have a nice time." He later said that he would like to tell the child that her prayer worked — and to thank her!

BREAKING
THROUGH

TUESDAY — FEBRUARY 13.

WHILE reading some inspirational thoughts, I came across this memorable little piece.

"I did!" said the wind.

"I did!" said the paper.

"I did!" said the string.

"I did!" said the boy.

In reality they *all* flew the kite. If the wind had stopped blowing, or the paper had torn, or if the string had caught in a tree, or the boy had fallen, then the kite would have come crashing down. To raise something off the ground, everyone needs to do their part and work together!

WEDNESDAY — FEBRUARY 14.

HERE is a thought for us to reflect upon today:

"If you love someone, tell them now, for hearts are often broken by words left unspoken."

THURSDAY — FEBRUARY 15.

FRANCIS of Assisi, when he was just an ordinary man, not elevated to sainthood, famously gave away his worldly goods to those in greater need. His philosophy of giving is perhaps best summed up in his prayer, "Lord, Make Me A Channel For Thy Peace":

Lord, grant me that I may seek to comfort
Rather than be comforted,
To understand than be understood,
To love than be loved,
For it is by giving that one receives
And by forgiving that one is forgiven.

FRIDAY— FEBRUARY 16.

THERE are times when most of us have a compelling desire to tell the world what we think of a certain person or problem, and other occasions when we realise that it would be wiser not to do so.

Each time I am tempted to let off steam, I am reminded of this advice:

"True wisdom is the skill to know just when to speak your mind and when to mind your speech."

As far as I know, the person who first wrote or spoke these few words has never been named, but they contain a wealth of wisdom.

SATURDAY — FEBRUARY 17.

A READER has sent me this centuries-old Celtic blessing on sleep:

May the angels watch me
As I lie down to sleep.
May the angels guard me
As I sleep alone.

Uriel be at my feet,
Ariel be at my back,
Gabriel be at my head,
Raphael be at my side.

Michael protect my soul
With the strong shield of love;
And the healing Son of God
Touch my eyes with blessedness.
                    Carmina Gadelica.

SUNDAY — FEBRUARY 18.

BELOVED, let us love one another; for love is of God; and every one that loveth is born of God, and knoweth God.

John I 4:7

MONDAY — FEBRUARY 19.

IT might be you just stopped to admire the colour of the sky or perhaps you did a good turn for a stranger. Maybe supper was nicely prepared and just what you liked most, but whatever the circumstances, you find you are ending the day with a small sense of satisfaction.

The poet John Dryden summed it up rather well when he said:

Happy the man, and happy he alone,
He who can call this day his own —
He who, secure within, can say:
Tomorrow do thy worst, for I have lived today!

TUESDAY — FEBRUARY 20.

IN a magazine devoted to the interests of our senior citizens I read an interesting item about those of maturer years and how they are treated in other parts of the world.

In Bermuda, older people are issued with a small, laminated pass. This entitles the holder to various concessions such as free travel. What I particularly like about this idea is that the pass is embossed with the words "Special Person".

We owe so much to these members of society and that is surely a thoughtful way of recognising the fact.

WEDNESDAY — FEBRUARY 21.

MILLIE was telling me about her daughter, who is soon to leave secondary education. "The teachers," she told me, "have always made sure that pupils keep a 'Record Of Achievement' to take with them when they go. It's a book containing a note of all their successes, however large or small. I think it's an excellent idea."

So do I. And perhaps it's one which all of us might also consider adopting, whether we keep a diary or simply a mental record. Then next time we're tempted to feel gloomy about how little we seem to have accomplished, we need only look in our book or consult our memory bank to remind ourselves of just how much we've done, and how many things we have to be proud of.

Make sure you keep yours diligently!

THURSDAY — FEBRUARY 22.

CHURCH notices don't always get it right. Just look at these examples:

For those of you who have children and don't know it, there is a nursery downstairs.

The minister will preach his farewell message and then the choir will sing "Break Forth Into Joy".

Jane Brown and John Smith were married in the church last week. So ends a friendship that began in their schooldays.

We would like all parishioners to know that the cost of attending the Fasting and Prayer Weekend includes all meals.

OUTLOOK

FRIDAY — FEBRUARY 23.

WHEN Marie first talked of giving up her lucrative career in the city to help care for children in Romania, many of her friends and colleagues made no secret of their grave reservations.

"It got to the point where even I started to wonder if I wasn't about to make a huge mistake," confided Marie. "Then I came across some words by Matthew Arnold: 'Life is not having and getting, but being and becoming'. It was as if those words were written just for me."

There are times in everyone's life when we need to make bold decisions, and on such occasions I find that's a piece of wisdom well worth remembering. And how is Marie? She is apparently finding her new job hard work — but she wouldn't change it for the world.

SATURDAY — FEBRUARY 24.

VICTOR, at the age of eighty, returned from a visit to Canada to see his granddaughter and her family. He loved his holiday, and was particularly enthralled by the plane journey.

"What impressed me most," he told me, "was the fact that however thick the clouds appeared from the ground, once you got above them, the sun was still shining brightly in a clear, blue sky. I'll remind myself of that whenever I'm feeling a bit down. The sun never deserts us — it's just that it's not always visible."

And that's just as true of a different kind of Son entirely.

SUNDAY — FEBRUARY 25.

HUMBLE yourselves in the sight of the Lord, and he shall lift you up.

James 4:10

MONDAY — FEBRUARY 26.

HAVE you heard of Rev. John Brown of Haddington and his "Self-Interpreting Bible" which was first published in 1778? It was very popular in its day and many editions were sold.

This Bible had explanatory notes to help readers to understand the text, and some Victorian editions had beautiful, coloured illustrations with space to record family details.

John Brown would today be described as a disadvantaged child. Born in 1722 to poor parents, he was orphaned while young, and became a shepherd boy.

A great reader, and with an astonishing talent for languages, he taught himself Greek, Latin and Hebrew, for his dearest wish was to be a clergyman — "My soul was remarkably affected and drawn to God," he said.

To achieve his aim, John earned a living as a pedlar and self-educated schoolteacher, overcoming many obstacles along the way.

Rev. John Brown, clergyman, theologian, scholar, and linguist, died in 1787 in Haddington, where he had been a much-loved clergyman for thirty-six years. I'm sure that he would agree with Calvin Coolidge's words:

"Nothing in the world can take the place of persistence."

TUESDAY — FEBRUARY 27.

D O you believe in miracles? Well, when was the last time you saw one?

There's an old Eastern saying which goes: "It's not walking on the air that's the miracle but walking on the earth." Every day we are in a miracle we don't even realise — a blue sky, white clouds, green leaves, the curious eyes of a child — our own two eyes. All is a miracle.

When was the last time you saw a miracle? Remember, you are one.

WEDNESDAY — FEBRUARY 28.

I WONDER if your community is lucky enough to have someone like Joyce? She is the sort of person who, in times of trouble, is first to provide not only a sympathetic ear, but practical offers of help and support.

"When I was a child," she once confided, "I lived in a neighbourhood of low incomes and high unemployment. Nevertheless, we all knew that in times of trouble we could depend on one another. No-one had much in the way of worldly goods, but it didn't stop us offering whatever we could. I'm just carrying on the tradition and would never think of doing anything else."

Thank goodness for such community spirit, and long may it flourish. In the words of Henry Wadsworth Longfellow: "Give what you have. To someone, it may be better than you dare to think."

Sometimes the simple fact that a fellow human being cares is enough to ease the heaviest burden.

March

NEXT time you find yourself fretting about something, try to focus your thoughts on the oak trees in the forest and diamonds in the earth. Both have emerged from pressures — sturdy and strong. You can do the same.

JANUARY is some weeks behind us now. How many resolutions did you make? How many did you keep?

Here are a few lines for those of us who are tempted to say, "Ah, well. There's always next year.":

Dream not too much of what you'll do tomorrow,
How well you'll work another year.
Tomorrow's chance you do not need to borrow —
Today is here.
Talk not too much of some new endeavour
You mean to make a little later on.
Who idles now will idle on forever,
Until life is gone.
Swear not some day to break some habit's fetter
When this old year is passed away.
If you have need of living wiser, better,
Begin today.

Anon.

SATURDAY — MARCH 3.

WHEN Eileen was hesitating over whether or not to return to college as a mature student, few people showed support, and one or two even pointed out that "at her age" she was unlikely to get very far. But then she received a letter from a friend, an encouraging missive containing a piece of advice which finally persuaded her to go ahead.

Now, I'm happy to say, Eileen is well into her second year, and loving every minute. And the advice which helped her to make the decision? It was a quotation from the well-known writer George Eliot: "It's never too late to be what you might have been."

I think that's wisdom worth following, whatever path you wish to take in life.

SUNDAY — MARCH 4.

LET your light so shine before men, that they may see your good works, and glorify your Father which is in heaven.

Matthew 5:16

MONDAY — MARCH 5.

LORD, when on my bed I lie
Sleepless, unto Thee I'll cry:
When my mind works overmuch,
Stay the "wheels" with Thy soft touch.
Just a quiet thought of Thee,
And of Thy sweet charity;
Just a tranquil prayer and then
I will turn to sleep again.

Elizabeth Sutherland.

TUESDAY — MARCH 6.

THE American newspaper columnist Ann Landers was once asked to name the most useful piece of advice she could pass on.

"It is to expect trouble as an inevitable part of life," she replied, "then, when it comes, to hold your head high, look it squarely in the eye, and say, 'I will be bigger than you. You cannot defeat me'."

In other words, respond courageously and creatively to the situation that confronts you. Become bigger than your problem, and it will seldom defeat you.

WEDNESDAY — MARCH 7.

LIFE'S PATHWAY

A WAYFARER through all the world,
A traveller through time,
An everyday adventurer
With distant hills to climb.
A seeker and a wanderer,
A searcher for the truth,
A dreamer of a thousand dreams
Re-capturing lost youth.

So little time, so short a span,
So much to do and learn,
Exploring all the paths of life
As seasons swiftly turn.
A wayfarer through all the world
In everything we do,
In search of love and hope and joy,
Still seeking something new.
                                    Iris Hesselden.

THURSDAY — MARCH 8.

THE Holy Spirit has many names. The Greek term Paraclete is perhaps the most comprehensive as it can mean so many things — Comforter, Consoler, Companion and my favourite translation — Affirmer.

There are times when we feel we are little use to our families, in our daily work and to the world in general. The Holy Spirit doesn't see us that way. The Holy Spirit builds us up, always sees the good in us and stands by us in times of trouble.

There are lots of occasions in our lives when we need to be reassured and to know that each one of us is uniquely important to God. The Holy Spirit is there to affirm just that.

FRIDAY — MARCH 9.

IS there a recipe for a good and happy life? Here are some ingredients suggested by Robert Louis Stevenson:

To be honest;
to be kind;
to earn a little
and to spend a little less;
to make, upon the whole,
a family happier for his presence;
to renounce, when that shall
  be necessary,
and not be embittered;
to keep a few friends . . .

There is more, but that sounds a promising start, doesn't it?

WISTERIA

SATURDAY — MARCH 10.

RON is a very clever fellow, an expert in the field of computers. I met him one afternoon, putting a large box into the boot of his car.

"I'm going into town," he explained. "My computer has developed a fault and I'm taking it to be repaired." I sympathised, but he added philosophically, "Well, it is getting on a bit, these things wear out, they're changing all the time, and you have to keep them up to date."

Like all man-made things, I thought, they soon become obsolete. What a contrast, we both agreed, with God's world that surrounds us. His creations are permanent and we have so much beauty around us every day.

SUNDAY — MARCH 11.

FOR me to live is Christ, and to die is gain.

Philippians 1:21

MONDAY — MARCH 12.

JO, in the newsagent's, was humming as she served me one day. "Sorry," she said. "They played my favourite song on the radio this morning, and I can't get it out of my head. Funny, isn't it, how some music can be so catchy."

Thinking about her comments later, it occurred to me that it's not just music that can be "catchy". Good humour, courtesy, optimism can all be contagious — just as, alas, grumpiness and gloom can be.

Finding myself humming Jo's song all the way home, I resolved to be extra careful just what "tune" I may be passing on in future!

TUESDAY — MARCH 13.

OUR friends Christine and Andrew began to talk one day about friends and neighbours with whom they had lost contact in recent times.

Sadly, a busy life can mean that many of us lose a once-close link. Often the only evidence of a formerly-strong friendship is the reciprocal sending of a card at Christmas time.

Here, found in an old scrapbook of cuttings, is a verse which says so much in a few lines:

Time goes so fast, life asks so much
No wonder friends get out of touch.
But in our hearts, deep, true, unseen
Friendship stays forever green.

WEDNESDAY — MARCH 14.

THERE'S a man who owns a candle,
And a man who has a match;
They'd like to get together,
But alas, there is a catch,
For neither trusts the other
Not to steal the precious spark.
So blinded and divided,
They stay stranded in the dark.
So let us draw a lesson
From this sad, misguided pair,
And try our very utmost
To love and trust and share.
For with determination,
And faith in human worth
We'll light so many candles
As will brighten all the earth.

Margaret Ingall.

THURSDAY — MARCH 15.

THE makers of sundial inscriptions in days gone by tended to include rather serious thoughts such as *The shadow passes, the light remains*. My favourite sundial motto, however, might equally well be applied to my favourite people: *Let others tell of storms and showers, I'll only count the sunny hours.*

FRIDAY — MARCH 16.

MEISTER Eckhart, a medieval Dominican monk, had a gift of unique observations on ordinary, everyday things. His feelings on prayer made me stop for a moment and think. He said:

"If the only prayer you ever say in your whole life is 'thank you', that would suffice."

SATURDAY — MARCH 17.

HERE is a traditional Irish toast to share, a favourite in the days before, during and after 17th March, St Patrick's Day:

*Always remember to forget
The things that made you sad;
But never forget to remember
The things that made you glad.
Always remember to forget
The friends who proved untrue;
But never forget to remember
Those who have stuck by you.
Always forget to remember
The troubles that passed away,
But never forget to remember
The blessings that come each day.*

SPRING
SPARKLE

SUNDAY — MARCH 18.

AND being made perfect, he became the author of eternal salvation unto all them that obey him.

Hebrews 5:9

MONDAY — MARCH 19.

THERE was a scientist who spent his entire working life trying to understand how it was that bumble bees could fly. The more research he carried out, the more frustrated he became, because according to all the data, bumble bees shouldn't be able to fly at all — they were just too heavy.

It was then he found faith in God, realising that in the end not everything could be explained and understood. Some things just had to be believed.

TUESDAY — MARCH 20.

THE English Civil War was not the easiest time to be a priest or a poet.

Thomas Traherne (1637-1674) was both of these and could have been forgiven for having a dim view of the world. Instead, he loved life and suggested that the problem lay not with the world but the way we looked at what he called "the mirror of infinite beauty".

"Your enjoyment of the world," he wrote, "is not complete until every morning you wake up as if in Heaven; see yourself in your Father's palace, and look upon the skies, the earth and the air as celestial joys with such an esteem as if you were amongst the angels."

WEDNESDAY — MARCH 21.

ONE Sunday the members of a small Highland church were discussing what their slogan might be. They came up with: "To be a family"; "Love God with all your heart and your neighbour as yourself"; and "There is no fear in love".

But the best statement came quite unexpectedly. One of the children attending Sunday school came running into the room during the meeting and said to her mother, "We've had a treasure hunt, and *I've got the treasure.*"

That became their slogan.

THURSDAY — MARCH 22.

OUR friend Alan said to me the other day, "You know, Francis, Margaret asked me this morning why I was wearing my old coat when I had a new one which was warmer and not so shabby."

Then Alan looked at me a little ruefully, and continued, "You know, I couldn't give her a reason, but when I thought about it I realised my old coat and I have known each other for a long time, and we are comfortable with each other. I know just how to turn up the collar at the right angle to keep out cold winds."

I nodded in agreement. What was it Victor Hugo said? "Old coats and old friends are the same thing."

Oh, yes, and so are old, comfortable chairs whose every creak is known and loved, and let's not forget much-read books. I like them all very much!

FRIDAY — MARCH 23.

"EXPERIENCE," I once heard someone say, "is what you get by not having it when you need it." I suspect a lot of us would have to agree with that remark, yet it isn't all bad news. It's true that experience can often come at a price but, once gained, how valuable it can be.

Auguste Rodin knew a thing or two about that. As a struggling young sculptor he applied three times to join the École des Beaux-Arts, only to be rejected on every occasion. Yet still he was able to say, "Nothing is a waste of time if you use the experience wisely."

I may not be a sculptor, but I'll definitely try to carve that philosophy into my life.

SATURDAY — MARCH 24.

LIKE many things in this world it depends how you look at it.

What am I talking about? Well, it was a line in a letter written by a friend who'd gone through some hard times. He'd been surprised by the people who had taken time to help him and equally surprised by those who hadn't.

"You know, Francis," he said. "When it comes to doing something for somebody, some folk stop at nothing."

SUNDAY — MARCH 25.

NOW the God of patience and consolation grant you to be likeminded one toward another according to Christ Jesus.

Romans 15:5

MONDAY — MARCH 26.

HUDSON Taylor, the famous missionary, was once asked if he didn't live a terribly hand-to-mouth existence.

"Yes," he replied, "but it's from God's hand to my mouth."

TUESDAY — MARCH 27.

HERE is an interesting extract from Great-Aunt Louisa's diary:

March 27th — "It has been a cold, roaring month, and I have sneezed, snuffled and coughed my way through the past week, feeling miserable. But a calm, sunny day brought a small joy to cheer me on my way today.

"Mid-morning I glanced out of the window, and there on the garden wall was a butterfly, beautifully marked in brown and orange. With wings fully spread, it was enjoying the gentle warmth of the sun. I don't remember ever seeing such a butterfly so early, the first, I hope, of the many which will enjoy my garden in the days to come.

"Winter ends. Spring comes with the promise of Summer, and we rejoice!"

Beside this entry is a small drawing of butterflies in flight and a spray of apple blossom.

Great-Aunt Louisa was ever the artist!

WEDNESDAY — MARCH 28.

YOU don't stop laughing because you grow old. You grow old because you stop laughing.

THURSDAY — MARCH 29.

THIS message was pinned above the desk of an American country doctor:
MY JOB:
To cure occasionally, to help frequently,
to comfort always.

FRIDAY — MARCH 30.

HERE is some valuable advice for every day of the week:

"Always keep your words soft and sweet, just in case you have to eat them. And never put both feet in your mouth at the same time, because you won't have a leg to stand on."

SATURDAY — MARCH 31.

JOAN was in a DIY shop, choosing paint for her kitchen. "It's not long since I last decorated," she admitted, "but I could see, almost at once, that I'd bought completely the wrong shade of green. In the end I decided it was worth the hard work to change it."

Fortunately Joan's mistake was not too difficult to correct, but it did set me thinking. Sometimes we realise we've made an error, yet choose to live with it rather than find the courage or make the effort needed to put it right. The consequences may affect only ourselves, but at times they can affect colleagues, friends and those we love most.

It's true that not all mistakes can be put right as easily as Joan's, but let's follow her example and resolve never to live our lives knowingly in the wrong shade of green!

April

SUNDAY — APRIL 1.

THEREFORE if any man be in Christ, he is a new creature: old things are passed away; behold, all things are become new.

Corinthians II 5:17

MONDAY — APRIL 2.

PATTY, who runs a Sunday School, is used to challenges, but admitted that even she had difficulties when one young charge asked her what a soul is. As she says, "On the face of it, this may not sound too difficult a question — however, just you try to answer it in simple words!"

Albert Schweitzer, the revered philosopher, doctor and winner of the Nobel Peace Prize, could have helped. "No-one can give a definition of the soul," he wrote. "But we know what it feels like.

"The soul is the sense of something higher than ourselves, something that stirs in us thoughts, hopes and aspirations which go out to the world of goodness, truth and beauty. The soul is a burning desire to breathe in this world of light and never to lose it — to remain children of light."

That's an explanation to inspire all of us.

TUESDAY — APRIL 3.

SPRING is pear and apple blossom seen against a blue sky. It is the flowering of primroses and small violets in all their fresh beauty, and yellow star-like celandines turning their faces to the sun on grassy banks.

Spring is birds nesting and daylight lengthening, thoughts of Easter, and washing flapping in a brisk breeze to blow away the cobwebs of Winter.

WEDNESDAY — APRIL 4.

VISITING folk in hospital can be a sombre affair, but our old friend Mary smiled when she saw this in a WRVS shop. The kind-hearted folk who voluntarily staffed the place obviously had a sense of humour. Pinned to the wall behind the till for all to see was a sign that said:

Lord, don't let us be like porridge, slow to get ready and hard to stir. Instead make us like cornflakes, always prepared and ready to serve.

Their sense of humour was more like a cup of tea — just the thing to relax you.

THURSDAY — APRIL 5.

GUARDIAN ANGEL

BE thou a bright flame before me,
Be thou a guiding star above me,
Be thou a smooth path beneath me,
And be a kind shepherd behind me,
Today, tonight and forever.

Elizabeth Sutherland.

FRIDAY — APRIL 6.

MIRIAM had an unexpected encounter with an old school friend one afternoon.

"As a child, Sally had been outgoing and confident and influenced me a lot," confided Miriam. "So it surprised me greatly when she told me that I, too, had influenced her! It seems she had always admired my tendency to think before speaking, and had done her best to emulate it."

Miriam's experience reminded me of the words of Carl Jung, who once said, "The meeting of two personalities is like the contact of two chemical substances: if there is any reaction, both are transformed."

It's rather nice to know that we can have such positive influence on the lives of others.

SATURDAY — APRIL 7.

I READ a charming poem called "The Old Man's Comforts (and how he gained them)". Written around 1800 by Robert Southey, a young man questions Father William on how he manages to remain hearty and healthy and not pine after his lost youth. Stanza by stanza, the wise old fellow answers the curious youth.

Towards the end the lad asks the older man why the declining number of days left to him don't seem to worry him more:

I am cheerful, young man,
Father William replied,
Let the cause thy attention engage;
In the days of my youth I remember'd my God
And He hath not forgotten my age.

SUNDAY — APRIL 8.

A ND go quickly, and tell his disciples that He is risen from the dead; and, behold, he goeth before you into Galilee; there shall ye see him: lo, I have told you.

Matthew 28:7

MONDAY — APRIL 9.

"F AITH and Hope triumphant say Christ will rise on Easter Day."

Surely the true essence of Easter is contained in these words, and don't they inspire joy and wonder, too? They come from "An Easter Carol" by Bishop Phillips Brooks (1835-93).

TUESDAY — APRIL 10.

F EW of us, I imagine, would consider that we've led a perfect life. However hard we may try, it's a rare soul who never regrets any decision they've made, deeds they have done — or even left undone.

Though I'm sure it's important to realise when we've got things wrong, I also happen to think that it's just as valuable to know when to forgive ourselves and to move on. Past errors can't always be erased, but we make a far worse mistake if we allow them to entirely overshadow the future. As I once read:

"Though no-one can go back and make a brand-new start, anyone can start now and make a brand-new ending."

And that's a destination that's well worth moving towards.

WEDNESDAY — APRIL 11.

MORAG Wilson, a senior citizen from East Ayrshire, and Lord Baden-Powell, the founder of the Boy Scouts — what could these two folk possibly have in common?

Well, let me explain. Morag had just heard of the death of an acquaintance.

"I hear Mr Nichol got away, then," she said, as if he was off on some long-delayed trip to a nicer place.

Earlier on the same day I had finished reading a biography of the Great Scout and found that on his gravestone in Kenya was inscribed a circle with a dot in the middle. This was Scout code for "Gone home".

What did Morag and Lord Baden-Powell share? Their faith. And in the face of such certainty, death holds no fear.

THURSDAY — APRIL 12.

THE Lady of the House had been to a talk at the village hall and came home full of enthusiasm.

"Our guest speaker was a forester," she told me, "and it was easy to see how much he loved his work. Yet one of the most thought-provoking things he said wasn't particularly to do with trees, but is in fact a Native American proverb: *We do not inherit the earth from our ancestors; we borrow it from our children.* Don't you agree that's a wonderful way to look at things, Francis?"

I do indeed — let's hope it's an acorn of wisdom that will grow and grow.

WATER BABIES

FRIDAY — APRIL 13.

I MET Laura as she was searching the shops for a gift for her new baby nephew. "Oh dear," she said, "there are so many things available — I'm having difficulty choosing. And yet there's one thing I'll give him which I know I can't find on the shelves."

I obviously looked intrigued, for she smiled knowingly. "Encouragement," she enlightened me. "It may be free, but it's invaluable. As the German writer Goethe once said, 'Treat people as if they are what they ought to be, and you will help them become what they are capable of becoming'."

It seems to me that Laura's nephew will be receiving a gift for life!

SATURDAY — APRIL 14.

LET me use you, normal day, and learn
from you,
And let me see the treasure that you are,
Never let me waste a single moment
Searching for a lost or distant star.

Let me bless you, normal day, before you leave
And hold you in a corner of my heart,
And let me make the most of all you offer
For very soon, I know you must depart.

The time goes by so swiftly, moments fly,
And all too soon the hours slip away,
And should I seek some perfect, bright tomorrow
I'll try to use you wisely, normal day.

Iris Hesselden.

SUNDAY — APRIL 15.

AND Mary said, My soul doth magnify the Lord, and my spirit hath rejoiced in God my Saviour.

Luke 1:46-47

MONDAY — APRIL 16.

THE guests at the Ambassador's dinner were all seated when a woman complained, "According to protocol, I should be seated over there."

The Ambassador smiled and courteously rearranged the seating.

Afterwards he was asked, "Does it not upset you when something like that happens?"

"Not at all," he replied. "I learned a long time ago that the ones who mind, don't matter, and the ones who matter, don't mind."

TUESDAY — APRIL 17.

THE graceful impala, a member of the African antelope family, can teach us a lot about treading carefully. They've been known to jump distances of eleven metres, and can leap to a height of over three metres, yet when placed in a zoo enclosure, surrounded by a low wall, they will never jump over it.

There's a very simple reason for this. These beautiful creatures simply will not make a move if they can't see where their feet will land. This way they won't find themselves on shaky ground.

This is something we should, perhaps, remember the next time we're tempted to leap before we look!

WEDNESDAY — APRIL 18.

IN 1918, A.D. Purvis opened a general store in Waller, Texas. He called it "God's Mercy Store". Every item on the shelves was clearly priced — with the price Waller had paid for it! Customers selected what they wanted and paid for it, adding on whatever profit they felt the shopkeeper deserved.

When Mr Purvis started the store he trusted that these transactions would provide enough to feed himself and his family. And they did, for over twenty years.

Most of us would aspire to pay an honest man his due. But how many would have the courage to put themselves in Mr Purvis' shoes?

THURSDAY — APRIL 19.

A YOUNG friend of ours is a real live-wire, forever on the move, organising, arranging and generally getting things done. When I smilingly asked him if he ever stopped, he laughed. "You know the proverb," he said. "Footprints in the sands of time are not made by sitting down!"

It was a new saying to me, and had clearly been taken to heart. It's good to see someone so eager to get on, but I hope Sandy doesn't forget to pause from time to time and simply enjoy the world around him. As a little rhyme goes:

Are you racing down life's highway?
Slow down a gear or two!
For you'll miss a world of wonders
If your dust obscures the view.

FRIDAY— APRIL 20.

HIS striking good looks and fine physique made Christopher Reeve the ideal actor for the role of Superman, the American fictional hero.

He looked set for a long and successful screen career when, thrown from a horse, he broke his spinal cord and was paralysed from the neck down.

He took up a new career as a fighter for disabled people, setting up a Paralysis Foundation and raising millions to fund research into spinal injuries.

In the nine years until his death at 52 in 2004 his courage and determination brought hope and inspiration to many, and he died knowing the work he had begun would go on.

A Superman indeed.

SATURDAY — APRIL 21.

SANDRA, who has worked for several charities and overseas aid agencies, has a personal motto she takes wherever she goes. She finds it as much help back home as she does in far-flung lands. It's the words of St John of the Cross and, like all truths, it's hard-hitting and to the point:

"Where there is no love, put love and you will find love."

SUNDAY — APRIL 22.

AS it is written in the prophets, Behold, I send my messenger before thy face, which shall prepare thy way before thee.

Mark 1:2

MONDAY — APRIL 23.

WHEN Ernest Shackleton made his heroic attempt to bring rescue to his stranded crew after their disastrous expedition to the Antarctic, he had the distinct impression that he and his two companions were not alone.

"When I look back on those days I have no doubt that Providence guided us," he later wrote. "I know that during that long and wracking march over the unnamed mountains and glaciers of South Georgia, it seemed to me that we were four, not three."

Likewise, we need not be alone in times of trouble.

TUESDAY — APRIL 24.

"CAREFUL — *that's expensive!*"
  The cautious cry comes loud,
"That ornament is fragile," or
  "No touching is allowed!"
Thank goodness for the beauty,
  Surrounding us for free —
The trees, the grass, the garden,
  The sun, the sky, the sea.
So many perfect marvels
  From which delight to take,
We taste and touch and smell them,
  And never fear to break.
I'll leave expensive knick-knacks
  To those who love them best,
Give me the world of nature and
  Let others keep the rest.

                    Margaret Ingall.

WEDNESDAY — APRIL 25.

NOT long ago I read these words: "It is only fair that he who seeks indulgence for his own faults should grant them in return."

Yes, charity not only in deed — but also in thought — helps the world go round.

The words are from the Roman poet Horace, a wise and tolerant man. They are surely worth remembering.

THURSDAY — APRIL 26.

THE Lady of the House read aloud an article in which a young actress said that she was dedicated to becoming exactly like a certain famous film star, and would try to copy her in every possible way.

This reminded me of what the much admired actress and singer Judy Garland said on the subject: "Always be a first-rate version of yourself instead of a second-rate version of somebody else."

Now, isn't that the wisest of ambitions, whether you are in the public eye or not?

FRIDAY — APRIL 27.

WISE words about when and when not to speak your thoughts came from Will Rogers, the American political sage and philosopher, who died in a plane crash in 1935. Here are two of his maxims:

"Never miss a good chance to shut up."

"Letting the cat out of the bag is a whole lot easier than putting it back."

LAKE LAND

SATURDAY — APRIL 28.

WE all tend to keep putting off until tomorrow tasks that should be done now. It's a tendency that has been with us for centuries, as I discovered when I came across these two thoughts in a book of vintage proverbs:

"Between saying and doing, many a pair of shoes is worn out."

Italian Proverb.

"The beginning is the half of every action."

Greek Proverb.

SUNDAY — APRIL 29.

FOR I am not ashamed of the gospel of Christ: for it is the power of God unto salvation to every one that believeth.

Romans 1:16

MONDAY — APRIL 30.

IF you know of someone who is in need of help, will you gladly give it? I'm sure most of us would.

But — and be honest — when you find yourself in trouble or in need, how happy are you to let others do for you what you would do for them? Sometimes accepting help can be the most difficult thing in the world.

The poet John Donne said, "As God loveth a cheerful giver, so He also loveth a cheerful taker, who takes hold of His gifts with a glad heart."

And who can doubt that a helping hand, from any quarter, is anything other than a gift from God?

May

TUESDAY — MAY 1.

GOOD manners teach us that in conversation one person should not do all the talking and another all the listening. We often hear someone comment, "I couldn't get a word in edgeways!"

I wonder if there are times when God feels the same way about us. We sometimes pray in such a rush — a waterfall of words — and then switch off again in a hurry.

Prayer is not just talking at God, it's talking *with* God.

WEDNESDAY — MAY 2.

THIS thought-provoking e-mail has been circulated around the world and a reader from Valdosta in Georgia passed it on to our friend Alison.

There are three types of Christians who respond to the call of service:

Rowboat Christians — they have to be pushed.

Sailboat Christians — they always go with the wind.

Steamboat Christians — they make up their minds where they need to be and go there regardless of the weather.

Which one are you?

THURSDAY — MAY 3.

FROM an early age Norah suffered from ill-health and, as a child, had to face several major operations. Now, as a young woman, she looks forward to the future with courage and optimism.

"I couldn't mope around feeling sorry for myself," she once smilingly explained. "To do that would be to let down all those who've helped me get this far."

You know, I suspect there are a lot of people like Norah in this world, ordinary folk who quietly get on with life, overcoming obstacles as best they can. As American poet Alice Mackenzie Swaim once wrote, "Courage is not the towering oak that sees storms come and go; it is the fragile blossom that opens in the snow."

How true, and how such blossom enriches the world.

FRIDAY — MAY 4.

I SEEK not the world's wealth but life's riches,
If it can be said of me that
I love fearlessly,
Dream passionately,
Give cheerfully,
Forgive freely,
Open my heart generously,
Laugh easily,
Speak truthfully,
And walk honourably,
Then I am rich indeed.

Rachel Wallace-Oberle.

LIFT HIGH
THE CROSS

SATURDAY — MAY 5.

OUR friend Pam met her nephew Jack and his mother one stormy day. The youngster was holding tightly on to two plastic handles.

"What are you doing?" Pam asked.

"Flying a kite," Jack replied.

Pam looked up into the sky but couldn't see anything except great, swirling clouds of mist.

"But how do you know there's a kite there?" she asked.

"Because every now and then I feel a tug," he answered.

For me, that's a perfect definition of faith. We believe in Someone we can't see, but believe He's there because He does answer us when we call on Him.

SUNDAY — MAY 6.

BUT Jesus withdrew himself with his disciples to the sea: and a great multitude from Galilee followed Him, and from Judæa.

Mark 3:7

MONDAY — MAY 7.

THIS thought stopped me in my tracks with the simplicity of its truth. If you find yourself brought down by where you live, the people around you or the environment you work in, here's a message for you from the philosopher Eusebius who lived in Caesarea in the third century B.C. He said:

"Remember, a sunbeam passes through pollution, unpolluted."

TUESDAY — MAY 8.

MALCOLM Muggeridge's book "Something Beautiful For God" tells of the work Mother Teresa and the Sisters of Charity did amongst the poor of Calcutta.

There was nothing beautiful in the squalid streets they walked, nothing beautiful in the conditions people were forced to endure. The real beauty shone out from the hearts of the women willing to do such work.

I was deeply moved when I read of the nuns gathering up the terminally ill from the streets and taking them to a place where they could at least "die within sight of a loving face".

It is in words and actions such as these, rather than all the scientific and technological advances of the world, that there is true hope for us all.

WEDNESDAY — MAY 9.

I DIDN'T feel inclined to talk
I had so much to do,
But someone seemed to need a word,
A friendly smile or two.

I really didn't have the time
For someone walking slow.
But as we strolled along, I found
A person nice to know.

So as the busy days pass by
I find it clear to see,
I must make time for everyone
As God makes time for me.

Iris Hesselden.

THURSDAY — MAY 10.

I WONDER if you recognise the name Jan Struther? That was the pen-name of Joyce Anstruther who, during the dark days of the Second World War, lifted national morale with her warm and humorous novel "Mrs Miniver".

She also wrote poetry, and composed the words of the much-loved hymns, "When A Knight Won His Spurs" and "Lord Of All Hopefulness". Like us all, Jan Struther knew difficult times but this never made her blind to other people's needs, as illustrated by her "Variation On An Old Proverb":

Hard words will break no bones
But more than bones are broken
By the inescapable stones
Of fond words left unspoken.

Let's try to make sure that we don't leave these unspoken.

FRIDAY — MAY 11.

S HELLEY called it "the moonlight-coloured May" while Robert Bridges described how "Spring goeth all in white, crowned with the milk-white May."

Hawthorn flowers have always delighted the poets, and little wonder. There are few sights more welcome than this magnificent display that marks the start of a new season.

It used to be looked on as a sign of the rebirth of life and people would remind friends of this by laying branches at their door. Yes, it is a joyous time when, as Tennyson put it, "the world is white with May".

SATURDAY — MAY 12.

HERE are two sayings about the power of music in our lives:

"When I hear music, I fear no danger. I am invulnerable, I see no foe. I am related to the earliest of times, and to the latest."

Henry David Thoreau.

"Music gives a soul to the universe, wings to the mind, flight to the imagination and life to everything." Plato.

SUNDAY — MAY 13.

LET your speech be alway with grace, seasoned with salt, that ye may know how ye ought to answer every man.

Colossians 4:6

MONDAY — MAY 14.

STEPPING STONES

NO-ONE likes to make mistakes
Or feel they've been a fool,
But those who never make mistakes
May never learn at all.
So don't get too discouraged or
Dwell harshly or too long
On bygone slips or blunders,
Or the times you got it wrong.
Just think of them as stepping stones,
You've passed and left behind,
They've paved your path to wisdom, so
Move on with peace in mind.

Margaret Ingall.

TUESDAY — MAY 15.

HERE is a prayer from the Dominican Republic to reflect the thoughts behind Christian Aid Week:

The sun offers its gift of warmth,
The sea offers its gift of water,
The mountains give their coolness and
   their beauty,
The breeze refreshes creation.
And we, too, bring our gifts so that all may
   have life.
Lord, use them to fill the world with peace
   and justice,
So that every home can have its daily bread.
                              Amen.

WEDNESDAY — MAY 16.

OUR friend Stuart passed on this tip about how we can make the most of each day.

"Some of us are morning people, and tackle our most challenging jobs before noon," he said. "Come afternoon, we may slump slightly and are not at our best. Others come to life right in the middle of the afternoon.

"Pace yourself. Also, don't aim for perfection every minute of every hour. Get to know your energy levels, and don't put off doing things by waiting to be 'perfect'."

A wise man once said: "Tackle the important tasks and duties the moment you feel 'good enough'. Remember, perfection is not possible — we have simply to do our best."

Good advice, I think you'll agree.

THURSDAY — MAY 17.

MY thought for today is about friendship and I hope that you enjoy sharing these words:
Not chance of birth or place has made us friends,
Being oftentimes of different tongues and nations,
But the endeavour for the selfsame ends,
With the same hopes, and fears, and aspirations.
These gentle, wise words which make such pleasing reading were written by Henry Wadsworth Longfellow, the famous nineteenth-century American poet.

FRIDAY — MAY 18.

WHAT is your goal today? It may just be to find time to go to the library for a special book. It may be a bit more ambitious: to tidy the garden, bake a birthday cake or visit a sick friend.
Goals — long-term and short — do matter. They give purpose to our lives. We may not always reach our goal but at least we will have tried. There is an amusing saying that sums it up: "Aim at nothing and you're sure to hit it!"

SATURDAY — MAY 19.

DARREN was talking about his work. "What a difference!" he told me. "My last boss never gave me any encouragement, never said thank you. My new one will say, 'Well done', and is helpful in every possible way. It makes such a welcome change."
So often a word of thanks or a little encouragement is all it takes to lift someone's heart, give them the spur to go the extra mile.

SUNDAY — MAY 20.

NOW I praise you, brethren, that ye remember me in all things, and keep the ordinances, as I delivered them to you.

Corinthians I 11:2

MONDAY — MAY 21.

I'M sure all of us occasionally wish we were other than who we are. We might like to be taller, slimmer, have different coloured hair, or any number of other things. But we often spend an inordinate amount of time worrying over what is, after all, only a tiny fraction of our life.

Ralph Waldo Emerson had some reassuring words on the subject and I'd like to pass them on:

"The roses under my window make no reference to former roses or better ones; they are for what they are; they exist with God today. There is no time to them, there is simply the rose — it is perfect in every moment of its existence."

TUESDAY — MAY 22.

IN the 1950s the Communist regime in Albania declared God illegal. Recalling how churches were destroyed and priests imprisoned, the Primate of Albania was later asked how close the state came to destroying the church.

"Well," he said, "you can destroy the forest, but the seeds will live on in the ground. And when the sun comes again the seeds will grow."

The oppressive rulers are long gone but God lives on, in the seeds in the ground and in the people's hearts.

WEDNESDAY — MAY 23.

WILLIAM Hazlitt wrote in 1826: "The art of conversation is the art of hearing as well as being heard."

Aren't these words wise? Think about them today.

THURSDAY — MAY 24.

OUR friend Marion attended a lecture where the speaker was an eminent consultant at a nearby hospital. One remark made a great impression.

"To keep mentally fit, forget about yourself at least three times a day," he said. "That can do more for you than a cart-load of pills and potions."

Not long afterwards, Marion's clergyman told his congregation how a positive attitude achieved through prayer is of great benefit. "Come to God first and then go out to face the difficulties of life," he suggested.

Combine these two pieces of advice and you might get something like this: think about God at least three times a day and you will find the strength to cope with the challenges that lie ahead.

FRIDAY— MAY 25.

I CAME on these words in an old book and thought how well they apply to us every day of the week:

"Our days are happier when we give people a bit of our heart rather than a piece of our mind."

SATURDAY — MAY 26.

PIPPA had been sewing a cushion cover as a present for her grandmother. It was made of patchwork pieces from the family "rag bag".

"It was lucky that so much material had been kept," she told us. "Do you know, this piece is from my mother's first dance frock, and here's another from the dress Grandma wore at her silver wedding celebrations. I had the idea," she explained, "after reading the words of an American writer called Christopher Morley:

'Cherish all your happy moments, they make a fine cushion for old age.' So I thought I'd take him literally!"

What could be nicer than a gift created with such affection sewn up inside?

SUNDAY — MAY 27.

BLESSED are the peacemakers: for they shall be called the children of God.

Matthew 5:9

MONDAY — MAY 28.

WE often take water for granted, turning on a tap time and again for the same priceless resource. I remember the first occasion I saw a fresh spring of water, spouting straight up from the ground.

I watched it for a long time, this free-flowing miracle. Little wonder that springs and wells become special places, revered and blessed. Since the beginning of time silver springs have been bubbling up from God's earth.

BUDS AND BLOOMS

TUESDAY — MAY 29.

HAVE you heard of Murphy's law? It goes something like this:

Nothing is as easy as it looks.
Everything takes longer than you think.
If anything can go wrong, it will.
I prefer to look at life this way:
Things are often easier than expected.
You could be surprised how quickly you are done.
If anything goes wrong — put it right.
Is that not a better creed?

WEDNESDAY — MAY 30.

OUR friend Edgar always has his feet firmly on the ground and his advice can be relied on, whatever the problem. Anyone experiencing anxiety or tension, he says, should keep these words in mind:

"You can't change the past, but you'll ruin the present if you keep worrying about the future."

THURSDAY — MAY 31.

THESE words are attributed to Charles I. Behind the trappings of royalty his trials and triumphs differed from yours and mine only in scale. He wrote "Upon A Quiet Conscience" for his own comfort but, centuries later, it is still relevant.

Close thine eyes and sleep secure,
Thy soul is safe, thy body secure;
He that guards thee, He that keeps,
Never slumbers, never sleeps.

June

THE great preacher John Wesley said: "He who governed the world before I was born will take care of it likewise when I am dead. My part is to improve the present moment."

One of my neighbours had a similar thought in mind when he hung this motto in his Summer-house which has doubled as a work-space and thinking-place for many years. It says:

I cannot be everywhere, so I'll do what I can here.
I cannot do everything, so I'll do what I can.
I cannot live forever, so I'll get started right now.

DID you know there is a patron saint of gardens and gardening? He is St Fiacre, an Irish monk who showed such a love of growing things that he was given land on which to build his own monastery and create a garden around it.

The size of the garden amazed everyone but he wanted it to grow all the flowers and herbs he needed. Many of the plants were for medicinal purposes and he used them to cure some of the ailments of the time.

He taught people how plants can heal both body and soul, a valuable lesson for us all.

SUNDAY — JUNE 3.

AND straightway the damsel arose, and walked; for she was of the age of twelve years. And they were astonished with a great astonishment.

Mark 5:42

MONDAY — JUNE 4.

TORRIDON in north-west Scotland is an area of dramatic mountains, clear blue lochs and sparse population. Despite its high rainfall Torridon is a magnet for thousands of walkers and climbers who prefer to sample the raw outdoors rather than spend their holiday on a crowded beach.

One visitor wryly observed, "There is no such thing as bad weather, only inappropriate clothing."

TUESDAY — JUNE 5.

I HAVE *found the sweetest bliss*
In simple little things like this:
A glossy blackbird on the gate
Singing blithely to his mate,
Bumble bees all plump and bold
Drifting through my marigolds,
Lilac bushes bent to earth
Boasting blooms of lavish girth,
An early rain upon the lawn
Glinting in the blush of dawn.
To my hushed, expectant soul,
Beauty speaks and makes me whole.

Rachel Wallace-Oberle.

WEDNESDAY — JUNE 6.

MIKE was rather taken aback when, visiting a factory on an industrial estate, he spotted these instructions on the staff notice-board:

Grumble
Criticise
Blame
Complain
Gossip
Think Negative

He was just about to ask the owner how, with these directions, he manages to run one of the most successful businesses in town when he caught sight of a single word at the top: "Don't!"

THURSDAY — JUNE 7.

GROWING old. It happens to most of us, so why do we worry about it? Perhaps we should see our later years as the nineteenth-century evangelist Hannah Pearsall Smith did.

"I always thought I should love to grow old," this remarkable lady wrote. "And I find it even more delightful than I thought. I seem on the verge of a most delightful journey to a place of unknown joys and pleasures . . .

"The world and our life in it does seem of too little account to be worth making the least fuss over when one has such a magnificent prospect close at hand . . . I am tremendously content to await quietly and happily the opening of the door that will let me in to my real abiding place. So you may think of me as happy and contented, surrounded with unnumbered blessings."

TRANQUILLITY

FRIDAY — JUNE 8.

AUDREY was a Land Girl during the Second World War. She has been an amateur actress, served on many community committees and has collected for many charities. Perhaps more importantly, Audrey has been a wife, mother and grandmother, a constant source of help and inspiration to everyone around her.

One day, she took a friend to a fund-raiser for the local Guides troop.

"Have you never considered being more of a shy, retiring type?" she was asked, more than a little tongue-in-cheek.

"When I stand in front of the Lord to account for myself, I want to be able to say I've no energy, enthusiasm, patience, love, kindness or compassion left. Every gift He gave me, I want to have used to the full," she replied.

SATURDAY — JUNE 9.

OUR old friend Mary's television was not working, so she had to telephone the manufacturer to report the fault. Automated telephone calls are not anyone's favourite way of passing the time, I'm sure, but having pressed various numbers in the correct order Mary was eventually connected to a real person on the other end of the line.

How different it is when we want to get through to God. No number to look up, no dialling and no waiting.

He's always there, ready to listen, whatever time of the day or night, whenever we need Him.

SUNDAY — JUNE 10.

AGAIN, the kingdom of heaven is like unto a net, that was cast into the sea, and gathered of every kind.

Matthew 13:47

MONDAY — JUNE 11.

IT has been well said that the person who never made a mistake never made anything.

Of course nobody likes to make a mistake, but here is one way of looking at it: if you make a mistake today you will be wiser tomorrow!

TUESDAY — JUNE 12.

AS DAY CLOSES

I LOVE the calm and quietness
At closing of the day,
A time for quietly being still
To meditate and pray.
For thoughtfully reflecting on
Each blessing one by one,
The folk we've met, kind words received
The things we've said and done.

A time for being thankful for
Our friends and families,
For all the good things we have shared
And special memories.
A silent peace steals over all
This is the hour of rest —
It seems a benediction falls
And I am richly blessed.

Kathleen Gillum.

WEDNESDAY — JUNE 13.

VAL had always wanted to visit Australia, often joking about her wish to experience life "upside down". The Lady of the House and I were not too surprised, therefore, when we finally received a postcard from her depicting a breathtaking view of the Outback at dawn, and bearing the following message:

I'm here, Down Under, having fun,
And isn't it just grand —
I've found the world looks just as fine
Whichever way I stand!"

I don't doubt it — the world is indeed a wonderful place, and aren't we lucky that we live in an age when it's possible to see so much of it?

THURSDAY — JUNE 14.

WHEN Barbara moved from a city flat to a cottage in the country, it was not without qualms. Her new home boasted a large garden, but she knew very little about how to look after it.

"However, I soon found it to be an asset rather than an a liability," she told me, "for as soon as my neighbours discovered my inexperience, they were happy to pause and chat. Soon I was being given not only advice, but seeds and cuttings. Now I feel settled in my new house.

"Not only did my garden prove a wonderful way of getting to know people, it's become something permanent for us all to enjoy."

I'm glad Barbara's move proved so successful. Sometimes a willingness to tackle something new can set the world blooming!

FRIDAY — JUNE 15.

IN his day Andrew Carnegie might have been the richest man in the world but his childhood was spent in poverty. He mixed with presidents and kings but never felt the need to excuse his humble Scottish birth.

"My mother — a nurse, cook, governess, teacher and saint, all in one. My father — exemplar, guide, counsellor and friend! Thus were my brother and I brought up. What had the child of a millionaire or nobleman that compared to such a heritage?"

SATURDAY — JUNE 16.

FOR many of us, reaching the moon still stands as mankind's greatest technological achievement. On the verge of that great step forward the people involved might have been excused for having a high opinion of themselves.

However, astronaut Frank Borman, as he orbited the moon in Apollo 8, had other things on his mind. Having travelled farther than any man in history, he was humble in the face of a higher power. In his prayer, broadcast on Christmas Eve 1968, he said:

"Give us, oh God, the vision to see Thy love in the world in spite of human failure; Give us the faith to trust Thy goodness in spite of our ignorance and weakness; Give us the knowledge that we may continue to pray with understanding hearts and show us what each one of us can do to set forward the coming of the day of universal peace."

SUNDAY — JUNE 17.

AND now, Lord, thou art God, and hast promised this goodness unto thy servant.

Chronicles I 17:26

MONDAY — JUNE 18.

THE Spanish philosophical writer Miguel de Unamuno wrote: "It is not the shilling I give you that counts, but the warmth that it carries from my hand."

Aren't these words perceptive and thought provoking? I think they were written by someone who understood that man does not live by bread alone.

TUESDAY — JUNE 19.

EACH of the US states has a state motto — "Eureka", in California, for instance. But the State of Ohio once had no motto, although it had a Latin one in the 1860s which had quickly fallen out of favour because it was one to which people couldn't relate.

Then in the 1950s a high school student by the name of Jimmy Masterdino had what seemed to him a brainwave — six potentially life-changing words.

He asked people to sign a petition to the State Legislature, thousands of names giving support, and it approved what has, since 1959, been the official state motto: "All things are possible with God."

An encouraging motto in any circumstances, isn't it?

WEDNESDAY — JUNE 20.

BOB was fortunate enough to spend many childhood holidays at the seaside, but never lucky enough to discover the pirate's chest of gold he dreamed of. Perhaps, he confided, that was why this little verse appealed to him:

You think you lack for treasure?
Just take a look around,
You'll find the world has riches,
Of taste and touch and sound.
They may not weigh your pockets
Like gems of worth untold,
But oh, they'll raise your spirits,
Much more than any gold!

THURSDAY — JUNE 21.

WE were once invited to a school sports day. It was fun to share the children's excitement, and I was intrigued when the Lady of the House remarked that the relay race always made her think of knowledge.

"You see, it's in the way that the things we know or learn get passed on to the next generation and the next," she explained.

"When any one of us discovers a new insight into something, or comes up with a scientific discovery, or something that improves the lot of ordinary people, the benefit gets handed on. And then that new generation builds on the knowledge and passes it on. Do you see what I mean?"

I did indeed. It's rather nice to think of human wisdom being passed on like a baton. And if we can each play our own small part, then it's one race in which we can all be winners!

FRIDAY — JUNE 22.

THE year is passing quickly by,
The days all come and go,
And what the months ahead will bring,
Lord, only You can know.
We thank You for companionship,
The laughter and the joy,
The gift of knowledge and of faith
Which nothing can destroy.

We ask for peace across the world,
With hope to light each day,
New tolerance for all mankind,
Lord, help us find the way.
We count our blessings many times
And all Your gifts we see,
Remind us, Lord, throughout the year,
The best is yet to be.

Iris Hesselden.

SATURDAY — JUNE 23.

EDWARD Thomas, born in Lambeth in 1878, was a poet whose finest verses were inspired by the English countryside and the people living in it. His best-known poem, "I Remember Adlestrop", describes a quiet railway station drowsing in the sun on a warm June afternoon.

This most peaceable of men enlisted in 1915, volunteering for action. When someone asked him why, he bent down, picked up a handful of earth and said, "For this."

He fell at the front, fighting for the land he loved.

ROSE COTTAGE

SUNDAY — JUNE 24.

AGAIN He said, Therefore hear the word of the Lord; I saw the Lord sitting upon his throne, and all the host of heaven standing on his right hand and on his left.

Chronicles II 18:18

MONDAY — JUNE 25.

BILLY Graham, the American evangelist, once said that the ability to laugh, share a joke and smile through our problems is a prime asset for us all.

"A keen sense of humour," he said, "helps us to overlook the unbecoming, understand the unconventional, tolerate the unpleasant, overcome the unexpected, and outlast the unbearable."

TUESDAY — JUNE 26.

THE simple press of a button, a flick of a switch, and we get what I'd call the "instant way of life". Or click the mouse beside a computer, and a letter can be delivered many thousands of miles away.

It is all modern progress but too often, observes our friend Jean, life seems to depend on forever trying to beat the clock. "When we slow down, we start to experience a real quality of life. It gives us a whole new perspective on what living is all about," she says.

I think that the author H. G. Wells put it well when he said: "We must never allow the clock and the calendar to blind us to the fact that each moment of life is a miracle and a mystery."

WEDNESDAY— JUNE 27.

IN 1850 a young man, Joseph Dobson, brought his new bride to Elland, Yorkshire, where he believed an inheritance awaited him. Alas, a dishonest solicitor had stolen the money and disappeared.

It was a bitter blow but the young couple had a brainwave: they would make cakes, biscuits and sweets and offer them for sale.

They sold them from their home, then opened a shop. Soon they had to build a factory and Joseph Dobson's later became a household name. Today many of Dobson's popular sweets are still made to old family recipes. The main one is surely good old-fashioned Yorkshire grit!

THURSDAY — JUNE 28.

WHEN we are ill it's all too easy to feel sorry for ourselves. John Donne, the sixteenth-century writer and poet would have had every reason to wallow in self-pity while seriously afflicted, but instead he wrote "The Devotions", which includes this uplifting passage:

"All of mankind is of one author and one volume. When one man dies, one chapter is not torn out of the book but translated into a better language, and every chapter must be so translated.

"Some pieces are translated by age, some by sickness, some by war, some by justice. But God's hand is in every translation and His hand shall bind up all of our scattered leaves again for that Library where every book shall lie open to one another."

FRIDAY — JUNE 29.

"**D**ADDY," said Sam, "I want a real, proper spaceship. Will you make me one?"

Chris couldn't help but smile when she overheard this request from her young nephew, yet it did leave her thinking. In childhood it's only natural that we expect a large amount of outside assistance to help us realise our dreams, but I wonder how many of us carry this idea through into our adult lives? Sometimes it's all too tempting to blame our failures on the shortcomings of others, rather than admit our own lack of effort.

As St Augustine pointed out, "God provides the wind, but man must raise the sails." So let's heed these words, plot our course with faith, and cast off with courage. We may not all reach the destination we aim for, but at least we can be sure that we won't make our journey unaided.

SATURDAY — JUNE 30.

CELTIC RUNE OF HOSPITALITY

*W*E *saw a stranger yesterday.*
  We put food in the eating place,
Drink in the drinking place,
Music in the listening place,
And with the sacred name of the triune God
He blessed us and our house,
Our cattle and our dear ones.
As the lark says in her song:
Often, often, often, goes the Christ
In the stranger's guise.

HAPPY HOLIDAYS

July

H E setteth an end to darkness, and searcheth out all perfection.

Job 28:3

M Y friend Henry, one of the keenest gardeners I know, once told me that his fine array of flowers and plants has inspired him to develop his own "Garden Of Daily Living":

First, plant three rows of peas:
   Peace of mind.
   Peace of heart.
   Peace of soul.
Next, plant four rows of squash.
   Squash gossip.
   Squash indifference.
   Squash grumbling.
   Squash selfishness.
Then — Plant three rows of lettuce:
   Lettuce be faithful.
   Lettuce be patient.
   Lettuce love one another.
Complete the operation by planting
   Thyme for each other:
   Thyme for family.
   Thyme for friends.

TUESDAY — JULY 3.

I BELIEVE the following came from a Quaker gentleman. I do not know his name but I pass on his words as an excellent route-map for life.

"If you take a few steps along a smooth, easy road and discover as you go that your mind is uneasy and your heart disturbed, turn back. This is not the way for you.

"But if, on the other hand, you are travelling along a road which is hard to the feet, which tests your strength and endurance, but you find that you are happy and assured, then continue along that road, for it is the way of God's choosing. The peace of God and the will of God go hand in hand."

WEDNESDAY — JULY 4.

DO you sometimes feel rather cross with family and colleagues? No? Well then, do you perhaps know someone who finds it easier to complain than to smile?

I found these words by an anonymous poet and perhaps you'd like to pass them on to someone who could use them:

What good did it do being grouchy today?
Did your surliness drive any troubles away?
Did you cover more ground than you usually do
Because of that grouch you carried with you?
If not, what's the use of a grouch or a frown
If it won't smooth a path, or a grim trouble
drown?
If it doesn't assist you it isn't worthwhile . . .
Your job may be hard but just do it —
and smile!

THURSDAY — JULY 5.

I SUSPECT we have all come across the sort of person who seems to think that the best way to improve the world is not by getting involved and helping, but by standing apart, and pointing out from a lofty distance just how humanity might improve itself. Louis Newman, who wrote this rhyme, thought differently:

I sought to hear the voice of God
And climbed the highest steeple,
But God declared, "Go down again,
I dwell among the people."

I think that advice is sound!

FRIDAY — JULY 6.

COME travelling along with me,
So much to do and so much to see,
And when you're seated in your chair
Then you can travel anywhere.
And if you have a favourite spot,
A special place you love a lot,
Then you can visit every day —
It's only just a thought away!

A mountain top near to the clouds,
A river bank, away from crowds.
A sunny beach with rolling tide,
The one you love close by your side.
A place to eat, a place to sleep,
Another memory to keep.
Come travelling along with me,
You'll find the road is smooth — you'll see!

Iris Hesselden.

SATURDAY — JULY 7.

OUR friend Greta saw this notice outside a church one afternoon when she was visiting a nearby town:

Be careful how you live. You may be the only Bible some people will ever read.

SUNDAY — JULY 8.

BUT the Lord of hosts shall be exalted in judgment, and God that is holy shall be sanctified in righteousness.

Isaiah 5:16

MONDAY — JULY 9.

THE first thing many of us do in a crisis is to switch on the kettle. A hot, soothing cup of tea shared with friends, or taken alone, never fails to lift the spirits. The writer of this poem, Rudyard Kipling, obviously knew how it felt to be without tea!

We had a kettle; we let it leak:
Our not repairing made it worse.
We haven't had any tea for a week . . .
The bottom is out of the Universe.

Another man of note who was fond of a good cup of tea was William Gladstone, the nineteenth-century British Prime Minister. He had this to say about his favourite brew:

"If you are cold, tea will warm you. If you are too heated, it will cool you. If you are depressed, it will cheer you. If you are excited, it will calm you."

TUESDAY — JULY 10.

"HERE'S a paradox for you, Francis," said the Lady of the House knowing my fondness for these apparently self-contradictory statements. "I've just come across this in a biography I'm reading, but the words are credited to our old friend, *Anon.*, who says:

"There is a wonderful, mystical law of nature that the three things we crave most in life — happiness, freedom and peace of mind — are always attained by giving them to someone else."

You know, I've often thought what a wise old being *Anon.* must be, and now I'm even more sure!

WEDNESDAY — JULY 11.

KIRSTY is an artistic girl who enjoys drawing, and is seldom seen without a paintbrush or a crayon in her hand. As her mother watched her draw one day, she was amused to see the way Kirsty carefully placed each crayon back in the box after she'd used it.

"It saves them getting lost," she explained, "and I always know where to find one when I want it."

Seeing all the colours blending together in the box reminded her mother of something she'd read: *We could learn a lot from crayons: some are sharp, some are pretty, some are dull, some have strange names and all are different colours, but they exist very nicely together in the same box.*

Such a simple illustration, yet one that should encourage us all to get on together, regardless of age, race or creed.

THURSDAY — JULY 12.

SOME years ago, the Lady of the House and I went to the seaside and, thanks to some gloriously sunny weather, we were able to sit beside the beach. Having spent much of that time watching a father and son building a huge sandcastle, we shared their regret as the inevitable happened, and the turning tide began to demolish it.

I was amused, however, to see that of all who viewed the destruction, it was the young lad who was most stoic. "Never mind, Dad," he consoled. "At least we enjoyed making it, and next time we'll know how to build one that's even bigger and better."

Now that is a wise young man. The ability to realise that painstaking effort is worthwhile is a gift to treasure.

FRIDAY — JULY 13.

HAVE you ever gone to bed wishing you'd done something different . . . or better? Or lain awake fretting about what the next day might bring? I'm sure we all do at one time or another.

The French writer and philosopher, Victor Hugo, had the perfect words for times like that. He said:

"Have courage for the great sorrows and patience for the small ones; and when you have completed your daily task, go to sleep in peace. God is awake."

How much reassurance there is in these last three words.

CRAFTSMANSHIP

SATURDAY — JULY 14.

HERE is a thought which seems to encapsulate the serenity of a perfect Summer's afternoon, written by the eighteenth-century English novelist Jane Austen:

"To sit in the shade on a fine day and look upon verdure is the most perfect refreshment."

SUNDAY — JULY 15.

FOR God so loved the world, that he gave his only begotten Son, that whosoever believeth in him, should not perish, but have everlasting life.
John 3:16

MONDAY — JULY 16.

THE broadcaster Howard M. Lockhart used to begin his programmes with a friendly greeting: "And how are you today?", stressing *you*.

I thought of this one day when our friend Angela mentioned the telephone "manners" of two acquaintances. Both had been so eager to pass on some items of local news that they spent all of twenty minutes recounting every last detail, overlooking the fact that Angela was obviously suffering from a heavy cold and a bad cough.

It is surely only good manners when introducing yourself on the telephone to enquire about the health of the person you are calling before launching into lengthy talk about yourself and others.

Let's try to remember this next time we call a friend with news that "just can't wait".

TUESDAY — JULY 17.

*MAY my prayers be like a tree
    Rising strong and true to Thee,
Crowned in humble beauty fair,
Fragrancing the very air,
Shading friends in need of rest
With gentle hope and quietness.*
                    Rachel Wallace-Oberle.

WEDNESDAY — JULY 18.

DID you know that gold is so long lasting that of all the gold ever mined, most is still in existence? It's also incredibly versatile — it can be made into blocks or the finest of wire, and just a small amount of this precious metal can be beaten out to cover three hundred square feet.

Gold is the only yellow metal, it can be so fine that light will shine through it and it will never rust. While there is no doubt that gold is precious the Bible tells us that there is something much more valuable:

"A good name is more desirable than great riches; to be esteemed is better than silver or gold."   *Proverbs 22:1*

So while we're right to cherish any gold we might own, we'd be wise to take special care of that most valuable of possessions, our reputation.

THURSDAY — JULY 19.

THE quickest way to receive love is to give; the fastest way to lose love is to hold it too tightly and the best way to keep love is to give it wings.

FRIDAY — JULY 20.

THE Lady of the House and I have in our bookcase a "Housewives' Guide" from some years ago. At the bottom of each page are words of wisdom which the publishers thought might help and inspire the housewife of the day. Many years have passed and fashions have changed since then but I think you'll agree there's still wisdom in these sayings:

Little deeds are like little seeds.
The great and the little have need of one another.
Walk swiftly from temptation lest it overtake you.
Think of ease — but work on.
Nothing is impossible to a willing heart.

SATURDAY — JULY 21.

OVERTURE

THERE'S no other sound like the song
of the dawn,
The first shining notes in the first glow of morn,
The stir of the earth as it wakens anew,
The tremble of grass at the touch of the dew,
The trill of the bird as it takes to the wing,
The thrill in the air as the world starts to sing.
All life is assembling, convening to play
An overture fit for the start of the day.

Margaret Ingall.

SUNDAY — JULY 22.

SHE saith unto him, Yea, Lord: I believe that Thou art the Christ, the Son of God, which should come into the world.

John 11:27

MONDAY — JULY 23.

FEELING a little frayed round the edges? Have you been rushing this way and that, doing many things and yet not seeming to achieve a lot? Well, take this centuries'-old advice from the Roman poet Ovid:

"Take rest; a field that has rested gives a bountiful crop."

So try again later — and see what you get done after a well-earned rest!

TUESDAY — JULY 24.

HERE are three thoughts to keep in mind today:

Remember that not getting what you want is sometimes a wonderful stroke of luck.

Remember that the longer you carry a grudge, the heavier it gets.

Remember that life's treasures are people, not things.

WEDNESDAY — JULY 25.

NOW, if you gathered together all the books which have been written trying to determine what life is about they would undoubtedly fill several libraries. Each author or philosopher would have his or her own take on the matter.

Herman Melville, the author of "Moby Dick", put a seafaring spin on the subject and I found a lot of comfort in his words.

"Life," he said, "is a voyage that's always homeward bound."

THURSDAY — JULY 26.

OUR friend Jenny offered us this thought one day:

"It is all right to have enthusiasm for 30 minutes, better still for 30 days, but it is the person who has it for 30 years who makes a success of life."

FRIDAY — JULY 27.

TOM and Caroline were married not long ago, and when I met Caroline she was brimming with pleasure at a late gift — a framed photo of their happy day, taken by her aunt and accompanied by a specially-written verse:

Snap! A picture caught in time
Within a flash of light,
A topper and a wedding gown,
Confetti fixed in flight.
A moment that will never dim
Held fast within its frame
A blushing bride, a handsome groom,
A vow, a change of name.
Behind the glass this happy scene
Is captured and displayed,
But deep within two loving hearts,
This day will never fade.

SATURDAY — JULY 28.

FEELING discouraged? Here's a thought to inspire you on the journey to greater achievement.

The task ahead of us is never as great as the Power behind.

SUNDAY — JULY 29.

AND immediately there fell from his eyes as it had been scales: and he received sight forthwith, and arose, and was baptised.

Acts 9:18

MONDAY — JULY 30.

ELEANOR ROOSEVELT, wife of the American President Franklin D. Roosevelt, toured the world making speeches. Here is one of her thoughts, worth passing on when somebody may be trying to discourage you:

"Nobody can make you feel inferior without your permission."

TUESDAY — JULY 31.

I'VE always cherished the verse in Isaiah 40 that says: "Those who hope in the Lord will renew their strength. They will soar on wings like eagles." It provides great comfort when we are facing hardship, with a promise that although life will bring its share of challenges, with God's help we will get through.

But did you know that an eagle can sense when a storm is coming, and rather than take shelter it will go to the highest point and wait? When the storm comes it will launch itself into the winds and soar above the raging tempest.

There's something very reassuring about the striking image of an eagle flying high in the sky, meeting trouble head on and rising above it. As Isaiah says, with God's help we will always be able to do the same.

August

WEDNESDAY — AUGUST 1.

I AM constantly amazed by how truly great beliefs and philosophies can best be expressed in a few words. And if you can make people smile, too, then so much the better.

These words by Sherry Keith really warmed my heart. "If God had a refrigerator," she wrote. "Your picture would be on it."

THURSDAY — AUGUST 2.

YOU can't be a rebel and go to church. After all, religion is for conformists, for folk who just want to go along with the flock.

You wouldn't have to search too far to find people who agree with these statements. And to them I say, "Well, then, what about Alice Cooper?"

Once famed for his shock-rock stage act, he is now a regular church-goer. And he finds his faith demands more of him than his previous hedonistic lifestyle ever did.

"People think it's ironic that Alice Cooper, this rock and roll rebel, is a Christian. But it's the most rebellious thing I've ever done. Drinking beer is easy. Trashing your hotel room is easy. But being a Christian — that's a tough call. That's real rebellion."

SUN BLESSED

FRIDAY — AUGUST 3.

" ALABASTER, jasper, amber, jet, quartz . . ."
Our friend Julia listened patiently as a friend's young son proudly displayed his fine collection of crystals and gemstones. She picked one up for closer inspection.

"That's a garnet," Matthew informed her without hesitation.

He was no doubt right, but it was hard to see any similarity between such a dull-looking specimen and the stone in the beautiful dress ring Julia is so fond of.

Of course, it took effort to turn the original stone into something beautiful. Stones may be tumbled, sawn, ground, sanded, polished or subjected to numerous other techniques to bring out their very best qualities. And though we might not always be aware of it, that's what life does to us as we face its many challenges.

As an old Chinese proverb says: "The gem cannot be polished without friction, nor man perfected without trials."

SATURDAY — AUGUST 4.

I ONCE asked a successful businesswoman what she considered to be her most significant achievement. Without hesitation, she answered, "My children."

I was filled with admiration that motherhood topped her list of priorities and she was unembarrassed to say so. The richest rewards are found not in accomplishments or possessions but in relationships.

SUNDAY — AUGUST 5.

I KNOW that Thou canst do everything, and that no thought can be withholden from Thee.

Job 42:2

MONDAY — AUGUST 6.

BY the wrought-iron wishing well
That's built with old grey stone,
I love to sit and idly dream
When I am on my own.
Where spears of blue delphiniums
Are standing tall and bold,
And honeysuckle tendrils wind
Their trumpets cream and gold.

Grasses whisper in the wind
As they sway gracefully,
And foxgloves nod their dainty bells
'Midst sage and honesty.
Hollyhocks and lupins make
A colourful display,
With rambling roses tumbling down
In beautiful array.

Are there fairy visitors?
I catch a glimpse of wings,
But maybe it's the butterflies
The Summer sunshine brings.
This magical secluded spot
Has caught me in its spell,
As I sit in this secret place
Beside the wishing well.

Kathleen Gillum.

TUESDAY — AUGUST 7.

I WONDER if you know this prayer which was first brought to my attention by a reader in St Andrews.

Purge out of every heart the lurking grudge. Give us grace and strength to forbear and persevere. Offenders, give us the grace to accept and forgive offenders. Forgetful ourselves, help us to bear cheerfully the forgetfulness of others. Give us courage and gaiety and the quiet mind. Spare us to our friends, soften us to our enemies.

Bless us, if it may be, in our innocent endeavours. If it may not, give us strength to encounter that which is to come, that we may be brave in peril, constant in tribulation, temperate in wrath, and in all changes of fortune, and down to the gates of death, loyal and loving to one another.

These are the words of the writer R. L. Stevenson, the much-loved "teller of tales". Born in 1850 in Edinburgh, he died in 1894 in Samoa.

WEDNESDAY — AUGUST 8.

BEFORE beginning his sermon a clergyman told a joke that made his congregation laugh. Two friends were arguing about who makes better coffee, men or women.

"My husband makes the best coffee in the world and that's the way it's supposed to be," one of them insisted. "There's a book in the Bible that backs me up."

"What book could that possibly be?" her friend asked in astonishment.

"He-brews!" the woman replied.

THURSDAY — AUGUST 9.

OUT with her dogs in local woods one Summer afternoon Tricia walked slowly up the hill towards a favourite beauty spot. Reaching the top, she could smell smoke and she caught sight of firemen desperately trying to contain a fire in tinderbox conditions.

Realising the danger she hurriedly retreated with her dogs to safety. The next day revealed the total devastation of nearly two acres; charcoaled tree stumps and saplings were a sad reminder of the blaze.

Gradually green, leafy plants and moss began to cover the burnt blackness and two years later a glorious sight could be seen. A purple red haze covered most of the once-affected area as a blanket of foxgloves bloomed everywhere between the charred tree stump remains.

Reflecting how, given time, Nature can heal itself, Tricia smiled, recalling the apt words of Dante Alighieri, the medieval Italian poet who said: "Nature is the art of God."

FRIDAY — AUGUST 10.

IT'S interesting to learn how others came to their faith. Jack had been verging on belief for some time when he read the works of the writer and philosopher Sir Francis Bacon. That great man had asked a simple question:

"Who taught the ant to bite every grain of corn she buries in her hill lest it should take root and grow?"

Jack realised there could only be the one answer.

SATURDAY — AUGUST 11.

"IT contains enough material to turn the world upside down and bring peace to a battle-torn planet. But most treat it as though it is nothing more than a piece of literature." Mahatma Gandhi spoke these words.

Emmanuel Kant described it as "the greatest benefit the human race has ever experienced". To Charles Dickens it was "the very best book that ever was or ever will be known to the world".

So what were they talking about? The Bible.

SUNDAY — AUGUST 12.

AND, behold, Boaz came from Bethlehem, and said unto the reapers, the Lord be with you. And they answered him, the Lord bless thee.

Ruth 2:4

MONDAY — AUGUST 13.

WITH the constant weeding and grass cutting at this time of year, do you ever wonder why we bother? Well, Dorothy Gurney's words might offer an explanation:

The kiss of the sun for pardon
The song of the birds for mirth
One is nearer God's heart in a garden
Than anywhere else on earth.

And when it's all done, I like to reflect on this, written by an anonymous gardener:

For only he knows perfect joy
Whose little bit of soil
Is richer ground than it was
When he began to toil.

TUESDAY — AUGUST 14.

THE Lady of the House saw these inspiring words outside a church one afternoon:
Does life get you down? Just look up!

WEDNESDAY — AUGUST 15.

IN his final days Sir Walter Scott cast his mind over the many volumes he had written and was comforted by the thought that, in his work, he had "tried to unsettle no man's faith, corrupt no man's principles and written nothing I could wish blotted out".

We may not be great writers but we can all aspire to follow his code.

THURSDAY — AUGUST 16.

THROUGH the years, friendships often become more precious. They are exquisite flowers planted in the gardens of our hearts, from tiny seeds they bloom to surround us with their beauty.

When the wind blows, we bow as one beneath the force of it. When the rain beats against us, we lean against each other. When the sun shines, we turn towards it and rejoice. We grow together, grateful for the company of one another.

Each flower in our gardens is unique. Some are flamboyant, others are less showy. All are unforgettable and the landscape they create is glorious.

These blooms do not wilt or fade and because of them we are firmly rooted, gently nurtured, and greatly blessed.

FRIDAY — AUGUST 17.

FOURTEEN-YEAR-OLD Jonathan wears a bracelet with the letters WWJD on it. When I asked him what it meant, he replied, "What Would Jesus Do?"

Charles M. Sheldon wrote "In His Steps" in 1896. His book asks the crucial question, "What Would Jesus Do?" and outlines what happens when several members of a church decide to ask this before making every decision. As a result their lives are transformed by God's power.

"In His Steps" has made a deep impression on many readers and WWJD has become one of the most widely recognised acronyms in Christian history.

Jonathan's bracelet is a tangible reminder for him to live with integrity and always apply prayer.

SATURDAY — AUGUST 18.

I ADMIRE folk who have boundless enthusiasm, and use it to get lots of different things done. I call them "action people".

Statesman Sir Winston Churchill was in this category, and never let a setback curb his passion for action. He was once asked to give his definition of the word "success", and he replied:

"Success is the ability to go from one failure to the next without losing your enthusiasm."

SUNDAY— AUGUST 19.

LET your heart therefore be perfect with the Lord our God, to walk in his statutes, and to keep his commandments, as at this day.

Kings I 8:61

MONDAY — AUGUST 20.

A N author once signed her book on the inside cover for me with these words: *We are shaped by what we love.*

Wisdom worth applying to each day's choices, don't you think?

TUESDAY — AUGUST 21.

"I KEEP my friends as misers do their treasure, because of all the things granted us by wisdom none is greater or better than friendship."

Just a few words but they are as true as when they were written by Pietro Aretino of Italy in 1537.

WEDNESDAY — AUGUST 22.

A FAVOURITE Scripture verse is Psalms 27:4 which says, "One thing I have desired of the Lord, that will I seek after; that I may dwell in the house of the Lord all the days of my life, to behold the beauty of the Lord, and to enquire in His temple."

To me it's encouragement to spend time with Him and discover and enjoy who He is. I think Thomas Blake must have felt this way when he penned these poignant words which I'd like to share with you:

Every morning lean thine arms awhile
Upon the window-sill of heaven
And gaze upon thy Lord,
Then, with vision in thy heart,
Turn strong to meet thy day.

THURSDAY — AUGUST 23.

DO you, like me, find that the most effective posters are those with the simplest words? Consider this one, pinned on the wall of a city office:

The shortest distance between two people is a long and happy smile.

FRIDAY — AUGUST 24.

*W*E wish them love to make them strong
For all they have to do,
We wish them wings to lift their hopes
And make their dreams come true.
We wish them many helping hands
When plans all go astray,
And ever more encouragement
To meet another day.

We wish them laughter and success
And all life has in store,
A cheerful mind, a happy heart
To help their spirits soar.
We wish them joy and peace and hope
To combat hurt or sorrow,
We wish them all a better world —
The children of tomorrow.

Iris Hesselden.

SATURDAY — AUGUST 25.

A CORRESPONDENT sent me this small but mighty quote:

Faith moves mountains; doubt creates them.

How very true!

SUNDAY — AUGUST 26.

O LORD, there is none like Thee, neither is there any God beside Thee, according to all that we have heard with our ears.

Chronicles I 17:20

MONDAY — AUGUST 27.

S OME years ago a painting by the famous French impressionist Henri Matisse was put on display in New York's Museum of Modern Art. It is thought that in over forty days, almost 116,000 people passed by "Le Bateau" before someone pointed out that it had been hung upside down!

It seems incredible that anyone could fail to notice the error, yet we often miss seeing what's in front of us, as our friend Karen discovered not long ago when her cousin visited from abroad.

On a tour of a town famed for its history and architecture, they made time to explore hidden alleyways, admire the buildings and enjoy the stunning views from the harbour. Two delightful hours sped by, covering a distance that normally takes no more than fifteen minutes.

All too often we hurry on our way, heads down, when we should really take time to look around us. Matisse would surely have agreed.

TUESDAY — AUGUST 28.

W HAT can give us comfort in times of trouble? Surely caring and love. As the Elizabethan poet and playwright George Chapman wrote, "Love is Nature's second sun."

Yes, and where would the world be without it?

SPREADING
HIS WINGS

WEDNESDAY — AUGUST 29.

A TEACHER asked her class to make drawings for the wall. She was walking round her pupils to see how they were getting on when she suddenly stopped.

"What are you drawing, Emma?" she asked.

"I'm drawing God," she replied.

"But nobody knows what God looks like!"

Without a pause Emma replied, "Well, they will in a minute!"

THURSDAY— AUGUST 30.

S UMMER isn't always quite
The way it's meant to be,
With cloudless skies and butterflies
And picnics by the sea.
For sometimes Summer days appear
Capricious as a queen,
They sulk and fret and never let
A glimpse of sun be seen.
But don't despair to see dark clouds
Or rainstorms passing by,
For every shower feeds the earth
And helps the plants grow high,
Let's just give thanks for every day
Albeit pearl or plain,
For not a rose would smell as sweet
Without the kiss of rain.

Margaret Ingall.

FRIDAY — AUGUST 31.

T HOSE who delight in trees understand Mother Nature's thoughts, speak her language and hear her heart.

September

DAWN SKY

I WATCHED the dawn make inroads through
  The chilly, vapoured air,
Erasing night's dark residue,
  Serene beyond compare.

There was, to my attentive eye,
  A sense of mystery,
Bewitching as the clouds sailed by
  In friendly gaiety.

With glowing pools of blue throughout
  This other-worldly place,
My racing heart, without a doubt,
  Found dreams in its embrace.

For, as the sun stood at the helm
  Of animated skies,
The fascinating heavenly realm
  Held hints of paradise.

                              Alice Jean Don.

THE law of the Lord is perfect, converting the soul: the testimony of the Lord is sure, making wise the simple.

                              Psalms 19:7

MONDAY — SEPTEMBER 3.

IN good time for the harvest season a correspondent sent me this quote from her church magazine which adds an extra dimension to the meaning of this time of year:

Wherever you go, no matter how unreceptive the soil, determine to spread heaven's seeds on earth. Invest generously and faithfully into the fields you walk, and you will be guaranteed the great wealth of an eternal harvest.

TUESDAY — SEPTEMBER 4.

I WAS privileged to share the last few hours of Andrew's life in this world with him. At times like these the vanities and trivial concerns of everyday life are put firmly in their place and, for a while, we are made starkly aware of the truly important things.

Andrew recited a prayer his mother had taught him as a child. It was simple. These words had suited Andrew as a child, as an adult and now at the end of his days — and will surely help each one of us each and every day.

"Please God, forgive me, and help me to start again."

WEDNESDAY — SEPTEMBER 5.

MANY have tried to describe just what it is that makes a mother special. I like these words by the American preacher T. Dewitt Talmage:

"Mother — she was the bank where we deposited all our hurts and worries."

THURSDAY — SEPTEMBER 6.

OUT of curiosity young Adam typed a word into an Internet search engine. In less than a second it found 63 million references to Jesus. He changed the word to God and found 160 million references.

It seems that even in the world of cyberspace the Lord is making His presence felt.

FRIDAY — SEPTEMBER 7.

IT'S official — at an eight-month study in College Station, Texas, it was proved that both women and men think better, generate more ideas and are more relaxed and content when they work in an office environment which includes flowers.

Seemingly, men have as much as fifteen per cent more ideas and women find more inspiring answers when there are plants and flowers nearby.

But, to be honest, many of us always knew that, didn't we? Isn't that why we take flowers to our sweethearts in mid-February, to our mothers in March and to our friends on their birthdays?

Don't we already know that flowers bring cheer to unwell friends, give comfort to the bereaved, help to say sorry to those we have offended and thanks to those who have been kind?

What is more heart-lifting than a woodland corner full of wild hyacinths? What is more touching than a daisy in a linked chain?

Whether wild or cultivated, in vase or hedgerow, there is nothing that can inspire us quite like a flower. As Jesus said, "Solomon in all his glory was not arrayed like one of these."

SATURDAY — SEPTEMBER 8.

IT has often been said that what's good and what's bad in life depends on your point of view. I once came across this short quotation: "Every path has a puddle."

Adults can take these words as a warning that nothing is perfect — but the Lady of the House knows a five-year-old with new Wellingtons who takes them as an exciting promise.

SUNDAY — SEPTEMBER 9.

FOR whosoever shall give you a cup of water to drink in my name, because ye belong to Christ, verily I say unto you, he shall not lose his reward.

Mark 9:41

MONDAY— SEPTEMBER 10.

NORMAN had been caught out. He confessed to me he'd been blowing his own trumpet and slightly exaggerated the part he'd played in an important business deal.

Sympathising with this all-too-human frailty I became aware of a nagging memory, a rhyme read many years ago, a warning against just this sort of situation. It went something like this:

If your lips you would keep from slips
Five things observe with care:
Of whom you speak, to whom you speak
And how and when and where.
If your ears you would save from jeers
These things keep meekly hid:
Myself and I and mine and my
And how I do and did.

TUESDAY — SEPTEMBER 11.

WHAT'S the point? After all, what difference will it make? It's the usual cry of those who perpetually put off doing even a little good because the world always seems to need so much more.

I once had it explained to me, not by a clergyman, not by a teacher, but by a friend as he patiently repaired his car's engine.

"Don't think of it as a drop of water in a vast ocean," Billy said. "Think of it as a drop of oil in an overheating machine."

WEDNESDAY — SEPTEMBER 12.

LEAVE IT TO GOD

I TRY to help the ones I know,
Each sad and troubled heart,
But in the lives of those I love
I only play a part.
I see the worry and distress,
The dreams that won't come true,
Lord, let me do the best I can
And leave the rest to You.

And in my own life, now and then,
When things are going wrong,
I tell myself You're always near
And You will make me strong.
So when the doubt comes creeping in,
As doubt will sometimes do,
Lord, let me do the best I can
And leave the rest to You.

Iris Hesselden.

THURSDAY — SEPTEMBER 13.

TWO Boy Scouts were asked by a leader to go and help another leader to erect a marquee.

"Oh, I don't think I know how," said one.

"I'll give it a go," said the other.

The words they chose spoke volumes about the youngsters and reminded me of this poem from our friend John's Scouting days:

Did is a word of achievement
Won't is a word of retreat
Might is a word of bereavement
Can't is a word of defeat
Ought is a word of duty
Try is a word for each hour
Will is a word of beauty
Can is a word of power.

FRIDAY — SEPTEMBER 14.

OUR old friend Mary was telling us about some of the advertisements which she has heard of in recent times. Here are a few lighthearted examples:

A Cumbrian fish and chip shop greeted potential customers: *Don't stand outside looking miserable, come inside and get fed up.*

A travel agent in Woking displayed a notice in large letters telling everyone who opened the shop door to *Go Away!*

A paint store in Coventry had a sign: *Brighten up your overcoat.*

Finally, a dry-cleaning firm in Barnsley insisted: *If it isn't becoming to you, it should be coming to us.*

SATURDAY — SEPTEMBER 15.

HERE'S a thought. Imagine the world was about to end and you only had time for one phone call. Who would you call? What would you say? Would you heal a hurt, reach out to comfort someone, forgive some long-held grievance?

Well, the world isn't about to end. But if that call was so important you'd give it your last few minutes — why wait?

SUNDAY — SEPTEMBER 16.

O LORD our Lord, how excellent is Thy name in all the earth!

Psalms 8:9

MONDAY — SEPTEMBER 17.

"CAN'T stop!" Joanne called out cheerily. "I'm just off to rehearsals."

I smiled as she hurried by, for Joanne is producing yet another play for local amateur players. She had, she once confided, always longed to be an actress yet soon realised that she just didn't have that kind of talent. "I was miserable at first," she told me, "but then I read some words by Charles R. Brown. He said:

" 'The white light streams down to be broken up by those human prisms into all the colours of the rainbow. Take your own colour in the pattern and be just that.' It soon made me realise that just because I'd never be a performer, it didn't mean I couldn't do anything else."

And judging by her popularity as a producer, I'm sure the actors are equally glad that she didn't let it stop the show going on!

TUESDAY — SEPTEMBER 18.

A BROOK beside my cottage
  Laughing down the hill,
Reminds me of the adage,
  "Oh, my soul be still."
Its gladness never varies
  Its waters never cease,
And the melody it carries
  Resonates with peace.

Rachel Wallace-Oberle.

WEDNESDAY — SEPTEMBER 19.

THE President of the United States was once on a hunting expedition in Mississippi. Things were not going well, but then he caught sight of a grizzly bear cub. It was so cute that he refused to shoot it.

When the press got to know, a cartoon appeared in the "Washington Post" which caught the attention of a Russian immigrant who ran a small novelty shop. His wife made a stuffed toy bear with button eyes and moveable limbs — it was soon sold.

Demand increased, and the craftsman wrote to the President asking permission to use his name. This was granted, and in 1906 the American toy-trade magazine "Playthings" coined the term Teddy Bear, enhancing the popularity of President Teddy Roosevelt and ensuring that many children and grown-ups have a cuddly toy from which they are reluctant to be parted.

All because the President refused to kill a baby bear!

THURSDAY — SEPTEMBER 20.

THERE can't be many of us who walk an entirely trouble-free road through this world. But take courage — those stony patches can be navigated. As American writer and pastor William Arthur Ward once observed: "We can throw stones, complain about them, stumble on them, climb over them, or build with them."

FRIDAY — SEPTEMBER 21.

SUSIE was what you might call a typical teenager. She liked chatting to her mother, often in the kitchen, usually when she'd had a less than successful day. One time, everything seemed to have gone wrong. She'd quarrelled with her best friend, forgotten to do her homework, and missed the bus home.

Her mother, busy baking a cake, listened carefully to the tale of woe.

"Here, try some of this," she said, handing her a bowl of beaten eggs.

"No, thanks," Susie replied.

"Well, what about some of this?" She handed her daughter a tub of margarine. "Or how about some baking soda?"

She smiled at her daughter's expression. "A lot of things don't seem good on their own," she said, "but put together, you find that they turn out all right. That's the way God works, too. We don't know why He allows some things to happen, but if we let him He can bring them all together and turn them into something special. We just have to trust Him."

SATURDAY — SEPTEMBER 22.

AN intellectual and spiritual giant, formidable scholar, brilliant writer, outstanding preacher and exemplary pastor. This is how people spoke of Glasgow's George Matheson and the tributes were all the more remarkable because he had been blind throughout his adult life.

He began his preaching career early, standing on a chair in front of the family at the age of seven, two strips of white paper representing Geneva bands at his neck. By the time he entered university aged 15, others had to read to him, but he had the heartiest laugh in the quadrangle and loved to sing — "John Peel" and "The Harp That Once Through Tara's Halls" were among his favourite songs.

He became something of a tourist attraction in his church at Innellan, visitors marvelling at his ability to memorise every word of a service. When he preached at Crathie, Queen Victoria had his sermon printed for circulation to her staff. He also learned Braille.

Writing "O Love That Wilt Not Let Me Go" took him, he said, less than three minutes and remains a firm favourite today.

SUNDAY — SEPTEMBER 23.

FOR in six days the Lord made heaven and earth, the sea, and all that in them is, and rested the seventh day: wherefore the Lord blessed the Sabbath day, and hallowed it.

Exodus 20:11

MONDAY — SEPTEMBER 24.

ONE afternoon twelve-year-old Thomas came home from school and discovered that the house keys weren't in their usual place. He tried to get in through the kitchen window, but it would only open a few inches.

Thomas could see a spare set of keys on a table, so he fetched a fishing line from the garage and tried to hook them through the window. They fell into the kitchen sink.

After twenty minutes, Thomas "caught" the keys and went to the front door. To his astonishment, it was unlocked. His "fishing expedition" had been completely unnecessary.

Thomas' family still laughs at this incident yet I think there's a moral to it. How many times do we assume that an open door is closed? Opportunities are all around us if we just take time to investigate them!

TUESDAY — SEPTEMBER 25.

WE speak of "horse sense" and in this context I read of a pony called Snowflake who, unusually for her, had refused to move from her position diagonally across the corner of her stable.

Her owner later discovered the reason. A family of new-born kittens lay buried deep in the straw in the corner of Snowflake's stable.

The animal had realised that the tiny creatures were in danger from the farmer's pitchforks, and she had been standing guard over her new-born friends.

WEDNESDAY — SEPTEMBER 26.

I READ a memorable quote from the American writer Edgar Doctorow. What he was talking about was writing a story without quite knowing how the tale would turn out, and it struck me that the words applied equally well to following your faith.

"It's a bit like driving along the road at midnight," he said. "You might never see farther than your headlights, but you can make the whole trip that way."

THURSDAY — SEPTEMBER 27.

SOMETIMES life seems big and scary,
Full of fears that loom unknown,
Thoughts of future days may daunt us
When we face them all alone.

Stop awhile and look around you,
No-one walks the world forlorn,
Friends and neighbours share the journey
Through this sphere in which we're born.

Hear each other's hopes and worries,
Share their joys and bear their loads,
Paths ahead will seem much clearer
When, with friends, you search for roads.

Let companions lend you courage,
Let their laughter cheer your day.
Love can conquer every shadow,
Lighting up the darkest way.

Margaret Ingall.

FRIDAY — SEPTEMBER 28.

THE American chat show host Johnny Carson interviewed Walt Jones — on his 110th birthday!

Mr Jones chatted about how people view age and "landmark" birthdays such as 40 and 50. Then he asked Mr Carson a question that so impressed me I'd like to pass it on to you.

"How old would you be if you didn't know the date you were born and there weren't no calendar to depress you once a year?"

SATURDAY — SEPTEMBER 29.

A COMPANION loves some agreeable qualities which a man may possess but a friend loves the man himself.

James Boswell.

Friendship and friends were important to James Boswell, the 18th-century Scottish laird and lawyer, writer and biographer.

Numerous books have been written about this man, who knew many of the important personalities of his day, and many readers, yesterday and today, have read and enjoyed Boswell's "Journal Of A Tour To The Hebrides", which he made in the company of his friend Dr Samuel Johnson.

SUNDAY — SEPTEMBER 30.

GIVE unto the Lord the glory due unto his name: bring an offering, and come before him: worship the Lord in the beauty of holiness.

Chronicles I 16:29

October

OCTOBER is a month of clear, cold, night skies, sprinkled with stars and frost-touched early mornings which make us appreciate sunny days. It is a month to enjoy delicious, newly-made bramble, plum and apple jams and jellies, not forgetting the delights of country walks.

It is a month of rustling drifts of fallen leaves and, although November is just around the corner, in more than a few gardens bright pink nerines — known to many as Guernsey Lilies — flower happily, tolerant of the unpredictable weather.

"There is no season when such pleasant and sunny spots may be lighted on and produce so pleasant an effect on the feelings, as now in October."

Thus wrote Nathaniel Hawthorne in his "American Notebooks". It is a sentiment with which most of us would surely agree.

I KNOW it's rude to jump a queue,
To push in all the while,
But if some stranger hesitates
Make sure you're first to smile!

Margaret Ingall.

WEDNESDAY — OCTOBER 3.

IN an effort to wean eight-year-old Josh away from the computer his father dug out his old toy soldiers and made his son a fort. It was soon a success!

Jeeps and trucks were added and Josh spent many hours fighting his imaginary battles. So much so that it was often a struggle to get the little fellow to say his prayers and go to bed.

Then Josh's father found some words by the French writer Baudelaire and he told his son, "There was a very wise man who wrote, 'A man saying his prayers is like a Captain posting sentries at night. After that he can sleep'."

Now the young soldier's prayers are said (dare I say) "religiously" and with military precision.

THURSDAY — OCTOBER 4.

WILLIAM Penn was an influential American in the formative days of the United States. He gave his name to the state of Pennsylvania and struggled to make sure it was founded on the principles of religious freedom. Along the way he wrote "The Fruits Of Solitude", from which came the following suggestions for changing your life for the better:

Think twice before speaking once . . . and you will speak twice as well. Rarely promise . . . but constantly deliver.

Do good with what you have . . . or it will do you no good.

Love is the hardest lesson . . . for that reason we should try hardest to learn it.

FRIDAY — OCTOBER 5.

ONE of our young friends has a tendency to go around complaining about this and that, seldom seeming to be happy with his lot. Now, imagine my surprise and delight one day when he told me of a printed notice he had seen while on holiday:

When you think the world has turned its back on you, take a closer look; it could be you who have turned your back on the world.

Somehow, I have the feeling that our young friend may be a lot happier about life from now on!

SATURDAY — OCTOBER 6.

IT'S not just the stirring tune which encourages us to sing "Onward Christian Soldiers" so heartily. The words, written by their clergyman as a processional hymn for the children of Horbury Bridge in Yorkshire, are truly a rallying-cry of faith.

In much quieter mood we sing "Now The Day Is Over", a complete contrast, yet both are from the pen of the Rev. Sabine Baring-Gould, born in Exeter in 1834. He spent much of his early life in Europe and succeeded his father as squire of Lew Trenchard in Devon, where he became rector.

He was a man of inexhaustible versatility and industry. Not only a theologian, but musician, folklorist, antiquarian and novelist, of whom it was said he had more works attributed to him in the British Museum catalogue than any other writer of his time.

Heartwarming enthusiasm indeed.

SUNDAY — OCTOBER 7.

BUT Jesus beheld them, and said unto them, With men this is impossible: but with God all things are possible.

Matthew 19:26

MONDAY — OCTOBER 8.

IN the busy rush of modern life it is often difficult to find time to be alone and to be still. Blaise Pascal said that all the troubles of life come upon us because we do not sit quietly for a while each day.

Thoreau loved being alone, saying he "had never found the companion that was as companionable as solitude".

Another philosopher said that solitude is to the mind what diet is to the body.

Of course we all love our family and friends and good company, but we also need time to ourselves, "space" as we might call it today.

TUESDAY — OCTOBER 9.

THE LIGHT OF HOPE

*H*OPE *may find it hard to shine*
When everything seems dark,
And gloomy prospects may define
Attempts to make their mark,
And yet whatever may befall
In Life's kaleidoscope,
Here's a challenge for us all —
Keep bright the light of hope.

John M. Robertson.

WEDNESDAY— OCTOBER 10.

MAISIE was reading a letter. "Oh, what wonderful news!" she exclaimed, flourishing the missive with a smile. "This is from my friend Rose. Her husband has just been promoted, and her daughter's been awarded a prize for athletics."

Maisie's delight was heartwarming, and I know she's not alone in such an attitude. As the poet Archibald Rutledge said: "One of the sanest, surest and most generous joys of life comes from being happy over the good fortune of others."

THURSDAY — OCTOBER 11.

LIFE is a journey. How often have we heard that said? But in a chaotic world it's often difficult to know which direction is best. The Russians have an old saying: "Go Godward, and thou wilt find a road."

Once you've been travelling a while you might start to have doubts. A man with his fair share of doubts and determination was Vincent van Gogh. He said, "Let your conscience be your compass. Though the needle sometimes seems to deviate, still one must try to follow its direction."

Later in life, when your strength is fading, these are Hindu words that offer hope: "The winds of God's grace are always blowing; it is for us to raise our sails."

And once the miles are walked and the work is done, "What better can the Lord do for a man," asks Charles Kingsley, "than take him home?"

FRIDAY — OCTOBER 12.

LIZA always sang out of tune. Sunday after Sunday, in the little church, she tended to put everybody else off. At every hymn her cracked voice rang out — flat.

Yet, strangely, when she died, the congregation missed hearing her.

The clergyman summed up their feelings. "She praised God in her own way," he said. "And if it was not always music to our ears, I am certain it was music to His."

SATURDAY — OCTOBER 13.

THIS is an ancient prayer with much to offer us in the 21st century:
Remember, O Christian Soul,
That thou hast this day,
And every day,
God to glorify.
Jesus to imitate.
A soul to save.
A body to mortify.
Sins to repent of.
Virtues to acquire.
Hell to avoid.
Heaven to gain.
Eternity to prepare for.
Time to profit by.
Neighbours to edify.
The world to despise.
Devils to combat.
Passions to subdue.
Deaths, perhaps, to suffer.
Judgement to undergo.

SUNDAY — OCTOBER 14.

LET brotherly love continue. Be not forgetful to entertain strangers: for thereby some have entertained angels unawares.

Hebrews 13:1-2

MONDAY — OCTOBER 15.

CRAIG has started secondary school. A big jump for him, but all the new faces, new places, and new lessons haven't bothered him one bit. I met him walking home one day with enough homework to keep him out of mischief for an hour or two.

"Ah, well," the young philosopher sighed. "You've studied geometry, so you'll know about angles, and the best way to deal with problems is always . . ?"

I hesitated, not wanting to show my ignorance.

"The try-angle," the little scamp laughed.

He'll go far, young Craig.

TUESDAY — OCTOBER 16.

SIMPLE words often express meaning better than a host of longer ones. This was proved to me when a friend who lives in Stockholm sent me this little-known Swedish proverb.

"Follow these tips, and we Swedes say that all good things will be yours," he wrote.

Fear less, hope more,
Eat less, chew more,
Whine less, breathe more,
Talk less, say more,
Hate less, love more.

WEDNESDAY — OCTOBER 17.

HAPPINESS and success, I was once reminded, can be achieved but only after travelling on a road of bumps and warning signs.

A wise friend told me: "The road will not be straight and easy. You will swerve on loops of Confusion, take jolts on bumps known as Failure, and halt at red lights called Enemies.

"Fortunately, you will glide through green lights called Family, have back-up spares known as Determination, forge ahead with an engine known as Perseverance, and enjoy good insurance called Faith."

And, at the end of the day, signs should welcome us to a place called Success.

THURSDAY — OCTOBER 18.

IT'S always the same in our gardens, isn't it? After a spell of windy Autumn weather, leaves are blown everywhere. It's hard to know just where to start clearing up. Then, suddenly, there'll be a change of direction, a new wind will blow and often we'll find the leaves have been whipped up in neat piles — well, almost! — against a wall in the corner of the garden.

Life can be just like that. Sudden change can spill into our lives and bring a chaos that seems insurmountable. But often if we wait, life will settle down, order will return and perhaps everything will be even better than before.

We should always, as the American aviator and explorer Richard E. Byrd said, "Give wind and tide a chance to change."

FRIDAY — OCTOBER 19.

OUR old friend Mary was talking one day about people who talk too much, take little action, and keep wishing they could locate that mythical hoard of gold at the end of every rainbow.

I quoted to her these words by an unknown writer: "Some people develop a wishbone where their backbone ought to be!"

SATURDAY — OCTOBER 20.

I FIRST read the words many years ago but it was some time later that I found a use for them. Let me explain.

Out walking with Callum we saw Kenny and his family. I mentioned I hadn't realised he was back in town. Then Callum grabbed me by the arm and we crossed the road to avoid his one-time friend.

He explained that twenty years ago Kenny had let him down badly and left town shortly thereafter. As both men were in their forties I reflected that the incident had happened half a lifetime ago. Many things had changed; not least that Kenny was a husband and father now.

Later, I shared with Callum some advice from George Bernard Shaw: "The only man who behaved sensibly was my tailor. He took my measurements anew each time he saw me, while all the rest went on with their old measurements and expected them to fit me."

Callum listened, and nodded. I doubt if he'll cross the road next time.

SUNDAY — OCTOBER 21.

AND hope maketh not ashamed: because the love of God is shed abroad in our hearts by the Holy Ghost which is given unto us.

Romans 5:5

MONDAY— OCTOBER 22.

I'D like to share this Celtic Mother's Parting Blessing with you which is as meaningful today as when it was first written many centuries ago.

The blessing of God be to thee,
The blessing of Christ be to thee,
The blessing of Spirit be to thee,
And to thy children,
To thee and to thy children.

The peace of God be to thee,
The peace of Christ be to thee,
The peace of Spirit be to thee,
During all thy life
And all the days of thy life.

The keeping of God upon thee in every pass,
The shielding of Christ upon thee in every path,
The bathing of Spirit upon thee in every stream,
In every land and sea thou goest.

TUESDAY — OCTOBER 23.

HERE are two descriptions of friendship which were new to me, and how true they both are!

Friendship is like a circle or a ring, it goes forever and has no ending.
Friendship is the only rose without any thorns.

GOLD LEAF

WEDNESDAY — OCTOBER 24.

I'M sure that, like me, you admire older folk who, blessed with good health, don't seem to feel their age. Bert is one of them, but he has made a discovery. He told me about it when I met him out walking.

"I never realised I was growing old," he chuckled, "But do you know how I found out?"

I shook my head.

"Because everybody has started telling me how young I look!"

THURSDAY — OCTOBER 25.

THE night is approaching
  Long shadows now creep;
Through meadow and woodland
  The dark stretches deep.

Up in the sky
  The stars burn all pearl-white,
And out from the hill edge
  The moon climbs quite milk bright.

Villages shine
  Like clusters of fish
In a vast shadowed ocean
  With only one wish.

To float to the morning
  So far out of view —
Safe, sound and sleeping
  Till the sun is made new.

Kenneth Steven.

FRIDAY — OCTOBER 26.

DURING a walk in the hills Fred took a detour to visit a Pictish burial site. Thousands of years ago large, rectangular monoliths were placed at four corners of the grave then the whole construction was shielded by a large slab laid on top of the four pillars.

The slab is still much as it was, but countless centuries of wind and rain have taken their toll on the supports. Each of these once-proud guardians has weathered away until they are nothing more than rough and irregular cones. But still they continue to provide support.

It occurred to Fred that the sides and outer corners, which served no real purpose, had flaked and fallen, but the pinnacle of each stone, where most of the weight lay, still held true. And each of the bases, where all the massive weight of pillar and slab were carried, were still as wide as ever.

Let's think of those ancient stones the next time we feel snowed under.

SATURDAY — OCTOBER 27.

HERE are some wise words for us to consider today, written by Cicero, the famous orator and philosopher whose life coincided with the fall of the Roman Republic:

Anyone who has a library and a garden wants for nothing.

SUNDAY — OCTOBER 28.

FOR where your treasure is, there will your heart be also.

Matthew 6:21

MONDAY — OCTOBER 29.

PROFESSOR William Barclay had five great principles to save us from the dangers of wealth.

We should ask ourselves, he said, how did we get our money? How do we regard money? How do we use money? Remember, money is always less important than people and giving money is not necessarily enough.

There are times when the giving of oneself is the greatest gift of all — for that is the gift Jesus gave to us.

TUESDAY— OCTOBER 30.

WHAT do you look for out of life? Success, promotion at work, moving to a bigger house, perhaps? All perfectly understandable, but what about the ability to lose yourself in the wonder of a daisy?

"If you get simple beauty and naught else," the poet Robert Browning wrote, "you get about the best thing God invented."

WEDNESDAY — OCTOBER 31.

THE Lady of the House once reminded me how, each and every day, we speak and write hundreds of words between getting up in the morning and retiring for the night.

Here's a thought to reflect on in this context:
A careless word may kindle strife:
A cruel word may wreck a life,
A timely word may soothe stress,
A lovely word may heal and bless.

November

*Y*OU *will never plough a field if you only turn it over in your mind.*

Irish Proverb.

ONE frosty Winter's evening our friend Pam was driving in the heart of the countryside when she saw reflected through her rear window a strange red glow in the sky. She stopped, got out and looked up.

The whole sky, pin-pricked with stars, was streaked with the red, green and silver lights of the aurora borealis, a breathtakingly glorious sight.

Every so often we all need to look up at the stars. Only two galaxies — the Milky Way and Andromeda — are visible to the naked eye. The former contains five hundred billion stars, and the latter, only a blob of light to us on earth, is home to half a trillion stars. These neighbouring galaxies are only two of one hundred billion galaxies swarming with stars.

Frightening? Amazing? Inconceivable? All of these, and all God's work, all in His care. As Elizabeth Barrett Browning wrote:

"Earth is crammed with heaven, And every bush aflame with God."

SATURDAY — NOVEMBER 3.

IN his youth Alan Anders travelled overseas to work on re-building Germany after the Second World War. Not only did he fall in love with the country and want to stay there but he also met Krista, the woman who would become his partner for life.

Alan and his wife celebrated their fiftieth wedding anniversary a few years ago. After heaping praise on Krista he ended a letter to a friend with this memorable German saying:

"An old man loved, is a Winter with flowers."

SUNDAY — NOVEMBER 4.

AND Jesus looking upon them saith, With men it is impossible, but not with God: for with God all things are possible.

Mark 10:27

MONDAY — NOVEMBER 5.

FRIENDSHIP is a garland
Embracing all mankind,
It's woven with affection,
With willing heart and mind.
It's twined with love and kindness
And care for common need,
It shines with all the colours
Of every race and creed.
So let us strive together
To bind it strong and sure,
And keep the garland glowing
To last for evermore.

Margaret Ingall.

TUESDAY — NOVEMBER 6.

DAVID SIMPSON was the village baker in Bathgate. He had seven sons, all of whom went into the bakehouse to work in the family business when they were old enough.

That is, except Jamie, the youngest. His brothers felt that he especially warranted a good education, and they resolved to club together to pay whatever it cost. So Jamie went to Edinburgh University as a teenager, and later qualified as a Doctor of Medicine.

He became one of the foremost physicians of his day and pioneered the discovery of chloroform, describing it as "one of the greatest discoveries ever made in medicine", saving thousands of lives and first used during an operation in 1847.

Queen Victoria appointed him her Physician in Scotland, and six years later when she gave birth to her fourth son, was prescribed chloroform.

We continue to remember today the importance of James Young Simpson, who was knighted in 1866. His achievements were made possible by those who gladly sacrificed their prospects for his.

WEDNESDAY — NOVEMBER 7.

IN this season of short days, drizzling rain and chill winds it's all too easy to have a "down" day. It's then I remember these words by C.S. Lewis and think of Springtime, both the earthly version and the heavenly.

"Think of yourself as a seed, patiently wintering in the earth; waiting to come up as a flower in the Gardener's good time, up into the real world, the real waking."

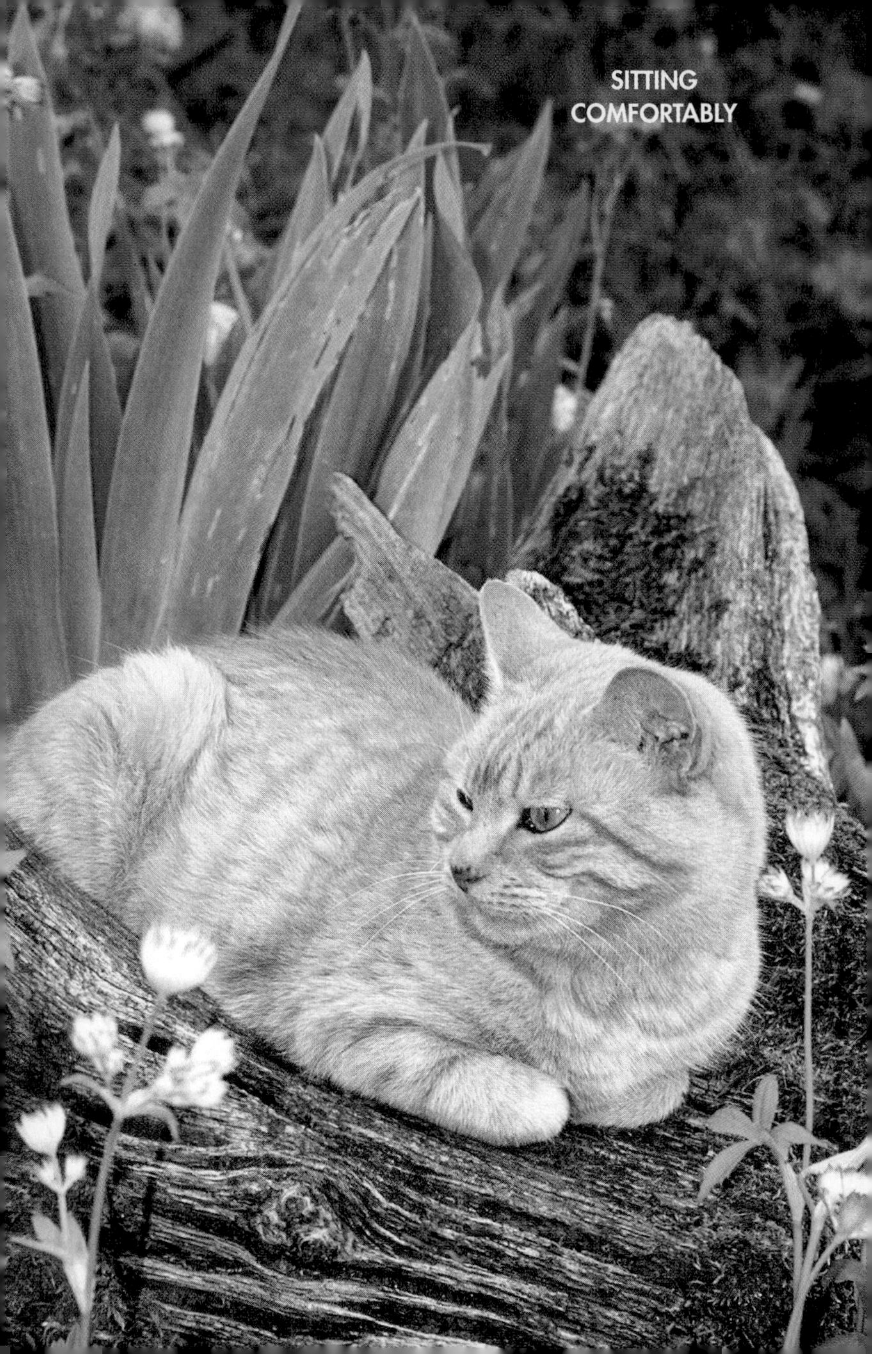
SITTING
COMFORTABLY

THURSDAY — NOVEMBER 8.

EVENING THOUGHTS

IF angels ask you what you did,
What you achieved today,
Would it be hard to answer them
And just what would you say?
We can't accomplish mammoth tasks,
Small jobs we need to do,
But, maybe, you just lent a hand
Or shared a smile or two.

Perhaps you sent a greetings card
Or simply made a call?
By lifting someone's heart and mind
You left them walking tall.
So, as the day fades fast away
And you lie down to rest,
You'll hear the angels whispering,
"Well done, you did your best."

Iris Hesselden.

FRIDAY — NOVEMBER 9.

IN his day few men understood the universe like Galileo. His real wisdom was to look for wonder, not only in the vastness of space or in the minute detail of the everyday world, but in both at the same time.

The majesty and intricacy of Galileo's world were summed up in these words:

"The sun, with all those planets revolving around it and dependent upon it, can still ripen a bunch of grapes like it had nothing else in the universe to do."

SATURDAY — NOVEMBER 10.

AS a child our friend John remembered going to the theatre to see "A Midsummer Night's Dream". It was a small audience that night, and his father's laughter dominated the auditorium, so much so that the actors played up to his obvious enjoyment.

John looked across at him and was surprised to see tears coursing down his cheeks. It was the first time he realised that you could laugh and cry at the same time.

There are so many reasons for tears — sad memories, diappointment, pain — but tears can also flow when we experience great joy.

A clergyman once said to me, "How fortunate are those who are able to cry. Some of us can't shed one tear even though we are crying inside.

"Believe me, there is nothing more painful than to be dry-eyed in the midst of great suffering or great joy. If you are lucky enough to possess it, give thanks to God for the gift of tears."

SUNDAY — NOVEMBER 11.

GO ye therefore, and teach all nations, baptising them in the name of the Father, and of the Son and of the Holy Ghost.

Matthew 28:19

MONDAY — NOVEMBER 12.

THOUSANDS of candles can be lighted from a single candle, and the life of the candle will not be shortened. Happiness never decreases by being shared.   Buddha.

TUESDAY — NOVEMBER 13.

WHO hasn't made mistakes? Which of us, if we had the chance, would not go back to make a few corrections? Of course we can't do this, but there is an alternative.

In her poem "The Land Of Beginning Again" Louise Fletcher wrote:

I wish that there were some wonderful place
Called The Land Of Beginning Again
Where all our mistakes and all our heartaches
And all our selfish grief
Could be dropped like a shabby old coat by
    the door
And never be put on again.

There's no such place, you say. But there's always a chance to put things right. There's a Land Of Beginning Again coming along later today — or tomorrow morning — if you want it enough, and if you miss that, there will be another one along the day after.

WEDNESDAY — NOVEMBER 14.

IN "Genius Of Electricity" Henry Ford recalls visiting a business acquaintance in California with Thomas Edison, the subject of his book.

Their host asked them to sign his guestbook. As well as names the book had columns for "home address", "occupation" and one headed "interested in . . ."

The great car maker watched as Mr Edison duly signed. In the final column he wrote without an instant's hesitation: "Everything".

Surely the best way to really live a life!

THURSDAY — NOVEMBER 15.

SEVERAL summers ago, near neighbours planted a miniature tree in their large front garden. Its trunk was thin and strangely crooked and a friend, who had stopped by, remarked, "Why would they bother with that tree? It will never grow."

I'm not sure why my neighbours chose that particular tree; perhaps they felt sorry for it in the nursery, but they lavished it with care. Gradually, over many months, its trunk began to straighten out.

Today, a hardy tree is flourishing and I'm reminded of life. When we generously love those who are different or don't seem to fit in, the results are often unexpected and beautiful.

FRIDAY — NOVEMBER 16.

THE writer Charles Lamb had a life beset by tragedy but when a friend, in a fit of despair, wrote to him saying, "the world seemed drained of all its sweetness," he was able to reply:

"Honey and the honeycomb, roses and violets are yet in the earth. The sun and moon yet reign in heaven, and the lesser lights keep up their pretty twinklings.

"Good humour and good nature, friends at home that love you and friends abroad that miss you — you possess all these things, and more innumerable; and these things are all sweet."

These words were true two hundred years ago. Look around you. Aren't they still?

SATURDAY — NOVEMBER 17.

THE old story about Pandora tells how she was sent to earth with a box which she had been instructed to guard but never open. Curiosity got the better of her. She lifted the lid and out escaped all the evils and sorrows of mankind.

What is often forgotten is that something remained safe inside the box. What was it? It was hope and it has been here to see us through all our troubles ever since.

That is the real lesson of the myth of Pandora's Box.

SUNDAY — NOVEMBER 18.

BEHOLD, I stand at the door, and knock: if any man hear my voice, and open the door, I will come in to him, and will sup with him, and he with me.   Revelation 3:20

MONDAY — NOVEMBER 19.

WALKING through a London graveyard Dave Harvey's eye was caught by a neglected stone in memory of a cavalryman who had won the Victoria Cross in the Charge of the Light Brigade.

Shocked that a hero's resting place was so poorly marked, Dave determined to locate and record the grave of every single Victoria Cross, a huge task for there are well over one thousand.

An accident in France left him in a wheelchair but he carried on and when he died, aged only 58, he left a massive two-volume work, "Monuments To Courage", testimony to his own unselfish dedication.

TUESDAY — NOVEMBER 20.

JOE'S one of a vanishing breed. In a world where lots of folk jump in the car and head to the out-of-town supermarket for their shopping Joe still brings groceries to the end of many a street in his mobile grocer's van.

He has an amazing talent for remembering customers' names. He never fails to ask them how they and their families are, and will always err on the side of generosity when bagging sweets for children. This verse was a present from Joe's dad when he handed the business down to his son:

You've got to have the goods, my boy,
If you would finish strong.
A bluff may work a little while,
But not for very long.
A line of talk all by itself
Will seldom see you through.
You've got to have the goods, my boy,
And nothing else will do.

"And it doesn't just apply to groceries," Joe says with a smile.

WEDNESDAY — NOVEMBER 21.

IT was a message from one friend to another inside a book found at a bring-and-buy sale:

If nobody cared just a little for you,
And nobody thought about me,
And we all stood alone in the battle of life,
What a dreary old world it would be!

The sale was to raise money for needy folk. So in the spirit of the verse our friend Ella bought the book. And a few more besides.

THURSDAY — NOVEMBER 22.

ALISTAIR was at a staff training seminar in a place he'd never visited before. His lunchtime stroll one day wasn't as relaxing as he had hoped, with the noise of the traffic, the smell of exhaust fumes and people hurrying by.

So, on impulse, he stepped through a broken fence on to a grassy path. Soon he found himself in a wooded glade, surrounded on all sides by roads and houses but the trees blocked out the noise and even the air smelled sweeter.

Then he stopped. There in front of him, crouched low in the long grass, was a handsome, red fox cub carefully watching a butterfly. Alistair watched, mesmerised until, finally, the butterfly flew too high and the cub ducked into nearby bushes.

"We think we're important," Alistair remarked later to friends. "But while we're going to conferences, seminars and such like, all around us Mother Nature is quietly going about her own staff training. And let me tell you, these few moments were worth weeks of stress management."

FRIDAY — NOVEMBER 23.

OUR friend Shirley particularly liked the way a friend in Australia had signed off in an e-mail.

"When I read your letters, my heart always smiles . . ."

A fresh phrase to remember next time we write to friends and family.

SATURDAY — NOVEMBER 24.

LIFE can be hard, there's no getting away from it. But is that such a bad thing? Consider these words written by James Fitz-James Stephen on the building of one of the wonders of the 19th century.

"The 'Great Eastern' and her successors will perhaps defy the rolling of the Atlantic and cross the seas without their passengers feeling they have left the firm land. The voyage from the cradle to the grave may come to be performed with similar facility.

"Progress and Science may, perhaps, enable untold millions to live and die without a care . . . but it seems unlikely they will have such a knowledge of the great ocean, with its storms, wrecks, currents, icebergs, winds and waves, as those who battled with it for years together in the little boat."

SUNDAY — NOVEMBER 25.

HOLD fast the form of sound words, which thou hast heard of me, in faith and love, which is in Christ Jesus.   Timothy II: 1:13

MONDAY — NOVEMBER 26.

THE eighteenth-century poet and philosopher Johann Friedrich von Schiller wrote these memorable words:

"Only those who have the patience to do simple things perfectly will acquire the skill to do difficult things easily."

TUESDAY — NOVEMBER 27.

BANKERS and financial experts may offer us lots of advice. However, all the experts in the world seldom tell us how to spend one item that is more important than money. I call it "Our Time".

This invisible currency is the most important thing we can spend or save, and the wise person will put family concerns high in his or her time-spending priorities, as Barbara Bush, a former First Lady of the United States, advised.

"At the end of your life," she said, "you will never have regrets at not having passed one more test, not winning one more verdict, or not closing one more deal. But you will regret any moments of time that you have failed to spend with a husband, a friend, a child, or a parent."

WEDNESDAY — NOVEMBER 28.

MOST of us, I'm sure, will at one time or another have heard the hymn, "Amazing Grace". How many though, I wonder, know that the writer of that beautiful song, John Newton, was once an atheist and a slave trader?

Later in life, though, Newton dedicated himself to God and wrote many hymns. In his eighties, even with his health failing, he refused to rest from good works.

Then he left us, with words that should be remembered as long as his greatest composition is sung. He said, "My memory is nearly gone, but I remember two things; that I am a great sinner, and that Christ is a great Saviour!"

THURSDAY — NOVEMBER 29.

WHY be positive? Why be happy? Well, I'll let George Bernard Shaw explain.

"Better keep yourself clean and bright," he said. "You are the window through which you must see the world."

FRIDAY — NOVEMBER 30.

MOUNTAINS OF PRAYER

IN the mists of the slumbering dawn,
  White mantles of lace hung to air,
I rise from my sleep and begin my ascent
  To the Beautiful Mountains of Prayer.

It's a road called Devotion that leads me
  Through the field of Confusion and Cares,
But I will not retreat for I clearly see
  The Beautiful Mountains of Prayer.

I will stop for a moment of rest
  By the waters I find flowing there,
And I stoop to drink from the Lake of Faith
  That mirrors the Mountains of Prayer.

Thus refreshed I press onward once more
  Through the cool of the Alpine air,
Led on by the whisper of Someone who calls
  My heart to His own in prayer.

And as ever I find Him there waiting
  To His welcoming arms I repair,
And together we climb the hallowed heights
  Of the Beautiful Mountains of Prayer.

Rachel Wallace-Oberle.

December

MAKE A START

TWO pans do not make a cook,
Two words do not make a book,
But it's a start.

Two planks do not make a boat,
Two sleeves do not make a coat,
But it's a start.

Two notes do not make a song,
Two shorts do not make a long,
But it's a start.

Two steps do not make a walk,
Two hands do not make a clock,
But it's a start.

Setting off is half the fight,
And if you know it to be right,
Make a start!

Maurice Fleming.

BUT the hour cometh, and now is, when the true worshippers shall worship the Father in spirit and in truth; for the Father seeketh such to worship Him.

John 4:23

SNOWSCAPE

MONDAY — DECEMBER 3.

WHEN cold weather and snow set in, Ontario schoolboy Jay set up a bird feeder near the front porch. He was hoping to see the many varieties of birds which frequented the neighbourhood and nearby woods.

As the weeks passed, not a single bird visited the feeder. Finally, after chatting with a knowledgeable neighbour, Jay discovered that he'd purchased the wrong seed. He replaced it.

Several days later, the birds arrived. Bluejays, cardinals, chickadees, sparrows, finches, mourning doves, and wild canaries filled the yard with a dazzling display of colour, movement and sound.

Now, isn't that like life? Sometimes a minor adjustment can produce spectacular results.

TUESDAY — DECEMBER 4.

OUR old friend, Mary, try as she might, could not console a close relative who had lost her husband. Then she said that she herself had found great comfort in these words by Robert Louis Stevenson:

He is not dead this friend; not dead
But on some road, which mortals tread,
Gone some few trifling steps ahead . . .
Push gaily on brave heart; for while
You travel forward mile by mile
He loiters with a backward smile,
Till you can overtake;
And strains his eyes to search his wake
Or, whistling as he sees you through the break,
Sits waiting on a stile.

WEDNESDAY — DECEMBER 5.

O UR friend Olivia was invited to a lunch party to meet a Norwegian family who were on holiday. After the meal was over, the children, three little girls, rose from the table and each went up to their hostess, bobbed a curtsy and said in impeccable English a little prayer of thanks, then, "Thank you for my lovely meal."

That set me thinking.

Why, I wonder, do we confine Grace to mealtimes? Why not, for example, before and after a holiday or an outing to the theatre?

"For what we are about to receive . . ." or "For what we have received, may we be truly thankful" need not necessarily refer only to food.

THURSDAY — DECEMBER 6.

F EW people can be unaware of the important part Martin Luther King Jnr. played in the struggle for human rights. Born in 1929 and growing up in the southern states of the USA, he knew all too well the injustices perpetrated against the black community.

Remarkably, however, he never let violent persecution, or even the bombing of his home, sour his ideal of peaceful protest. "Darkness cannot drive out darkness; only light can do that. Hate cannot drive out hate; only love can do that," he once said.

Martin Luther King Jnr. didn't live to continue his struggle for a better world, but if we all follow his philosophy, who knows what progress we might yet achieve.

ETERNITY

FRIDAY — DECEMBER 7.

JILL was trying to cope with a piece of bad news when two of her neighbours called and helped to cheer her up.

"Remember, we're here to talk and share your concerns," they told her. "We're with you at this difficult time."

Albert Schweitzer put it perfectly when he wrote: "Sometimes our light goes out and is then sparked into flame by another human being. Each of us owes the deepest thanks to those who rekindle this light."

SATURDAY — DECEMBER 8.

I'VE always felt that one of the most important ingredients of a good friendship is tolerance, so I was pleased to receive the following poem. It was given to me by a neighbour, Hilary, who tells me it was written especially for her by her friend Wynne:

We may not always think the same,
My oldest friend and me,
And often, when we meet to chat,
We find we don't agree.
Yet still I'd hate to do without
Our natters over tea,
For one point that we don't dispute —
We're perfect company!

SUNDAY — DECEMBER 9.

I HAD rather be a doorkeeper in the house of my God, than to dwell in the tents of wickedness.

Psalms 84:10

MONDAY — DECEMBER 10.

TOMMY'S been a regular churchgoer all his days. He told me about a friend who had laughed at what he called Tommy's "blind faith".

"Oh, it's not that," Tommy assured him. "Over the years I've wrestled long and hard with my doubts."

"So how can you still say you believe if you have doubts?" the friend asked.

"Oh, well, that's easy," Tommy assured him, "You see, I have doubts about my doubts, too."

On hearing this I was reminded of some wise words from Francis Bacon: "If a man will begin with certainties," he said, "he shall end in doubts; but if he will be content with doubts, he shall end in certainties."

TUESDAY — DECEMBER 11.

A FAVOURITE beauty spot in the West Highlands of Scotland is known as the "Rest And Be Thankful". It's a spiralling road that climbs through spectacular hill scenery en route to the Atlantic coast.

Each time our friend Hamish travels this road, he's reminded how important the word rest is, and how thankful we should be for the opportunity to do so when we can.

I also recall the saying: "Rest tonight is best for tomorrow." With a good night's repose behind us we are duly recharged and refreshed for a brand-new day and its challenges.

"Sleeping sound makes the world go around," advises another saying. Now, isn't that the way to "rest assured" of a good day ahead?

WEDNESDAY — DECEMBER 12.

FRANK lives in a big city and had just returned from a holiday in a remote village. "How did the break go?" asked a friend.

It had been very enjoyable, and the experience which had most impressed Frank was when he was out late one evening and had observed the night sky with thousands of stars shining above. Back home, they were partially obscured by the bright street lights.

Now, isn't that a drawback to all our lives? The good, simple things are so often lost in the hurly-burly of a busy existence.

THURSDAY — DECEMBER 13.

LORD, for tomorrow and its needs,
I do not pray;
Keep me, my God, from harm of sin
Just for today.

Let me both diligently work,
And duly pray;
Let me be kind in word and deed,
Just for today.

And if today my tide of life
Should ebb away,
Take me to heaven to live with you,
Lord, today.

So for tomorrow and its needs
I do not pray,
But keep me, guide me, love me, Lord,
Just for today.

Elizabeth Sutherland.

FRIDAY — DECEMBER 14.

IN one of the darker periods of the world's history Victor Frankl was an inmate of Auschwitz and Treblinka. He saw many terrible things but his abiding memories of that time were of people, inmates no better off than others, who chose to comfort their fellow men and women.

They would, for example, give away the last of their bread to someone who could not possibly be hungrier than them.

"The way a man accepts his fate," he wrote, "and all the suffering it entails, the way in which he takes up his cross, gives him ample opportunity — even in the most difficult circumstances — to add a deeper meaning to his life."

SATURDAY — DECEMBER 15.

DURING the cold, early hours of Winter walking to work always seemed a difficult challenge for our friend Sheila until she came across a quote which filled her with a new sense of thankfulness. G. K. Chesterton once said:

"When we were children we were grateful to those who filled our stockings at Christmas time. Why are we not grateful to God for filling our stockings with legs?"

SUNDAY — DECEMBER 16.

AND she shall bring forth a son, and thou shalt call his name Jesus: for he shall save his people from their sins.

Matthew 1:21

MONDAY — DECEMBER 17.

MISTAKES . . . we all make them. And there's no denying it can be a painful process. If, like many of us, you have made one recently, here are a few encouraging words to keep in mind:

"He who never made a mistake never made a discovery."

Samuel Smiles.

"A life spent making mistakes is not only more honourable but more useful than a life spent doing nothing."

George Bernard Shaw.

Do you feel better now?

TUESDAY — DECEMBER 18.

IT'S all too easy to live for tomorrow, continuously putting things off but as these words translated from ancient Sanskrit show, today is, and always has been, a good time to focus on.

Look to this day! For it is the very life of life. In its brief course lie all the varieties and realities of your existence: the bliss of growth, the glory of action, the splendour of beauty. For yesterday is already a dream and tomorrow is only a vision, but today, well lived, makes every yesterday a dream of happiness and every tomorrow a vision of hope.

Look well, therefore, to this day. Such is the salutation of the dawn.

So why not start something useful today?

WEDNESDAY — DECEMBER 19.

IN the early years of the nineteenth century a Scottish family eked out a living in China. For entertainment they sang hymns in the evening.

The second son always requested "The Ninety And The Nine", in which Jesus brings ninety-nine sheep safely home, then searches the deserts and rocky places for the missing one. But every time they sang it he burst into tears.

It became so distressing that his mother refused to sing it unless he promised not to cry when they sang about the poor lost lamb. The little lad promised but, come the sad part, he turned away and cried silently.

That little lad was Eric Liddell, who would become an Olympic athlete and devote the rest of his life to missionary work. Until his death in a Japanese concentration camp Eric Liddell lived his life with one purpose — to bring just one more lost lamb safely home again.

THURSDAY — DECEMBER 20.

WATCHING the musician Evelyn Glennie play her percussion instruments, it is hard to believe she cannot hear a single note.

When she became deaf by the age of eight, people expected Evelyn to give up her dream of a musical career. Instead she learned to "feel" the music through vibrations and went on to become the world's most famous percussionist.

Evelyn's joy in the sounds she makes shines on her face and each day she gives thanks for finding a way to defeat what seemed an impossible obstacle.

FRIDAY — DECEMBER 21.

I'M always enthralled with Winter's enchanting transformation of our world and the way everything becomes lovelier when covered by snow. Here's a memorable quote for a midwinter's day by Samuel Taylor Coleridge.

"Advice is like snow; the softer it falls, the longer it dwells upon, and the deeper it sinks into the mind."

SATURDAY — DECEMBER 22.

CHRISTMAS is not far away, and I have chosen these lines for you today from my scrapbook.

As fits the holy Christmas birth,
Be this, good friends, our carol still —
Be peace on earth, be peace on earth
To men of gentle will.

Surely this reflects the true spirit of the season — peace on earth, a wonderful wish for the world. It was written by William Makepeace Thackeray, the Victorian novelist and journalist whose enduring classics "Vanity Fair" and "Pendennis" sit on our bookshelves.

A happy and peaceful Christmas to you all!

SUNDAY — DECEMBER 23.

AND when they were come into the house, they saw the young child with Mary his mother, and fell down, and worshipped him: and when they had opened their treasures, they presented unto him gifts: gold, and frankincense, and myrrh.

Matthew 2:11

MONDAY — DECEMBER 24.

THE time draws near the birth of Christ;
The moon is hid; the night is still;
The Christmas bells from hill to hill
Answer each other in the mist.

You will find these beautiful, tranquil lines on Christmas Eve in Tennyson's poem "In Memoriam". The year 1850 was important to the poet — he married, saw "In Memoriam" published, and was appointed Poet-Laureate in succession to Wordsworth.

"In Memoriam" was inspired by his friendship with Arthur Hallam which dated from their student days at Cambridge. Arthur became engaged to Tennyson's sister.

Born in Somersby Rectory in Lincolnshire in 1809, Alfred, Lord Tennyson, lived for poetry. Among his best-loved poems are "The Lady Of Shalott", "The Charge Of The Light Brigade", and "Crossing The Bar", one of his last poems.

TUESDAY — DECEMBER 25.

WHAT do you think of when you think of Christmas? Santa Claus? Decorations? A Christmas tree? Family parties? Cards and calendars? Brightly-wrapped parcels?

No-one will blame us for thinking about any of these, but let us try too to travel back in time, to find ourselves in a simple stable on a starry night and to see a young mother bend over her newborn child in a manger.

Do that and we really will be sharing in the joy and wonder of Christmastide.

WEDNESDAY — DECEMBER 26.

A GREAT deal of story and legend is attached to plants, and it is said that when the Magi, the three Wise Men from the East, arrived with their precious gifts of gold, myrrh and frankincense for the Christ Child, a poor shepherdess called Madelon was standing outside the stable. She was in tears for she had no gift for the baby Jesus.

An angel saw her tears, and gently brushed aside a soft blanket of snowflakes to reveal white Christmas Roses tipped with pink, a perfect gift for the Christ Child.

Christmas Roses are beautiful flowers which bloom and brighten our gardens in the cold and darkness of mid-Winter.

THURSDAY — DECEMBER 27.

IT'S a fact that almost all polar bears are born on or around Christmas Day. They're barely larger than the length of a human thumb.

Think of them this Christmas, beginning their lives amid the Arctic ice, such fragile bundles of white at the heart of the Winter storms.

FRIDAY — DECEMBER 28.

THESE words from the great thinker and inventor Thomas Edison are framed on the desk of a highly-successful company executive:

"Opportunity is missed by most people, because it comes dressed in overalls and looks like work."

A thought to ponder, wouldn't you agree, when the next job looks challenging.

SATURDAY — DECEMBER 29.

HOME is where there's someone waiting
When you need a kindly smile,
When you're feeling sad and weary,
And you need to rest awhile.

Home is where you'll find a welcome
With the love that someone bears,
Love that simply asks no questions,
But in all your burdens, shares.

Elizabeth Gozney.

SUNDAY — DECEMBER 30.

HEAVEN and earth shall pass away: but my words shall not pass away.

Luke 21:33

MONDAY — DECEMBER 31.

AS the year draws to a close we always receive a special "end of the year letter" from our friend Henry. One year his letter contained a little drawing of Old Father Time sitting rather disconsolately beside empty bottles, the nearest labelled December. Beside him were these lines by Thomas Hood from "For The New Year":

For hark! the last chime of the dial has ceased
And Old Time, who has his leisure to cozen,
Has finished the months like the flasks at a feast
Is preparing to tap a fresh dozen!

"I hope," Henry wrote, "Your own fresh dozen for the coming year are of the finest vintage!"

And the Lady of the House and I, in turn, wish you all the same — a happy and peaceful New Year to you!

Photograph Locations and Photographers

IN HIS FOOTSTEPS — *Jedburgh Abbey.*
BRIGHT LIGHT — *By Loch Rannoch, Perthshire.*
OUTLOOK — *Carnasserie Castle, Argyll and Bute.*
WISTERIA — *Broadway, Worcestershire.*
SPRING SPARKLE — *Near Pitlochry, Perthshire.*
FÊTE DAY — *Finistère, Brittany.*
LAKE LAND — *Loughrigg Tarn, near Ambleside, Cumbria.*
TRANQUILLITY — *The Oxford Canal at Napton.*
ROSE COTTAGE — *Adare, Limerick, Eire.*
HAPPY HOLIDAYS — *Penwith, Cornwall.*
HEARTLAND — *Burnsall, Wharfedale, North Yorkshire.*
AUTUMN'S ARRIVAL — *Bargany Garden, near Girvan.*
THE LINK — *Clachan Bridge, Isle of Seil.*
THE ROCKS REMAIN — *South Stack Lighthouse,
                          Holyhead, Anglesey.*
ETERNITY — *Beach, Abersoch, North Wales.*

ACKNOWLEDGEMENTS: **Matt Bain;** Buds And Blooms. **David Bigwood;** Eternity. **James D. Cameron;** Bright Light. **Paul Felix;** Wisteria, Tranquillity. **V. K. Guy**; Lake Land. **Dennis Hardley;** The Rocks Remain. **T. G. Hopewell**; Autumn's Arrival, Snowscape. **C. R. Kilvington;** Heartland. **Douglas Laidlaw;** Fête Day, Happy Holidays, Craftsmanship, The Link. **Oakleaf;** In His Footsteps. **Polly Pullar;** Making Tracks, Breaking Through, Sailor's Rest, The Highlander, Gold Leaf. **Sheila Taylor;** The Awakening, Spring Sparkle, Water Babies, Lift High The Cross, Rose Cottage, Sun Blessed, Sitting Comfortably, Merrily On High. **South West Images**; Spreading His Wings. **Iain White;** Outlook.

Printed and Published by D. C. Thomson & Co., Ltd.,
185 Fleet Street, London EC4A 2HS.
© D. C. Thomson & Co., Ltd., 2006   **ISBN** 1-84535-153-3